The Complete Book of
Picnics

Text and Photographic Concepts by
James K. McNair

Major Photography by
Tom Tracy

Art Direction by
James Stockton

Design by
Craig Bergquist

Drawings by
Ellen Blonder

Photographic Styling by
Lenny Meyer

Ortho
Books

Manager, Ortho Books
Robert L. Iacopi

Editorial Director
Min S. Yee

Editor
Marian E. May

Production Editor
Anne Coolman

Administrative Assistant
Judith C. Pillon

Additional
photography by
Dennis Bettencourt
Fred Kaplan
James K. McNair
Dick Rowan
Photo Credits,
page 112

Consulting Home Economist
Cynthia Scheer

Copy Editing by
Judith Whipple

Proofreading by
Editcetera
Berkeley, CA

Indexing by
Baxter & Stimson

Typography by
Terry Robinson & Co.
San Francisco, CA

Color Separations by
Color Tech Corp.
Redwood City, CA

Printed by
Kingsport Press
Kingsport, TN

Address all inquiries to:
Ortho Books
Chevron Chemical Company
Consumer Products Division
575 Market Street
San Francisco, CA 94105

The Complete Book of
Picnics

The World of Portable Feasts page 4

Setting the stage for festive
picnicking

Picnics American Style page 8

Around-the-World Outdoor Meals page 42

Any Time, Any Place page 62

Picnicker's Guide to Shopping and Planning page 86

Practical suggestions for buying,
preparing, packing and transporting picnic food and gear.

The World of Portable Feasts

Picnics, in the sense of eating outdoors, have been around as long as man has been on earth. Among history's famous portable feasts was Cleopatra's sumptuous banquet on the Nile aboard her golden barge carrying Anthony back to Egypt. Persian poet Omar Khayyam's picnic statement was less complicated — "A book of verses underneath the bough, a jug of wine, a loaf of bread — and thou . . . ."

Originally the word "picnic," from the French **pique-nique,** meant "a fashionable social entertainment in which each party present contributes a share of the provisions." (That's the modern meaning of "pot luck".) Today's definitions update the word picnic to describe "a pleasure party in which all partake of a repast out-of-doors," or "an outing or excursion, typically one in which those taking part carry food with them and share a meal in the open air."

The Complete Book of Picnics extends the basic meanings even further to include **any** meal — whether the simplest fare for one or the most superb banquet for a dozen — that is transportable from the kitchen or dining room. Thus, you have the portable feast, the mobile meal that takes you away from the dining table and makes you a **picnicker**, outdoors or in.

The Complete Book of Picnics presents dozens of feasts designed to inspire creative picnic experiences. Many are simple, homey ideas that can be put together at a moment's notice. Others are extravaganzas, creations of fantasy and adventures in outdoor (or indoor) eating.

Above: Outdoor feasters must be prepared for the unexpected, as we learned while photographing this book. In this case, Lin and Linda settled down for a leisurely afternoon meal in a bucolic setting, with dairy cows grazing lazily in the distance. Suddenly the dinner bell sounded and the herd headed for the barn, pausing to look curiously at the picnickers. Opposite: In a matter of minutes the pasture was total tranquility again, leaving the picnickers to enjoy their repast in solitude.

Food and Fun

You'll find that **The Complete Book of Picnics** is not only a cookbook but also a survey of fully developed events that often carry out a theme with recipes to match. The essential ingredient of our picnics is pleasure: the enjoyment of good food and pleasant activity in an attractive setting at any season, any time of day or night. We photographed picnickers on snowy mountain slopes, on warm beaches at dusk, in chilly autumn woods and in city parks in the rain.

To emphasize the fun of picnics at any time or any place, we encourage you to consider the coziness of a spread by your own fireplace or in an urban roof garden high above the city, in front of the Christmas tree, on a porch protected from a warm spring rain — all perfect places for food, friends and fun.

Left: Turn-of-the-century picnickers enjoyed outdoor dining in the good old summertime. Styles change, but good food, pleasant company and the great outdoors remain important elements in the world of picnicking. Below: Today, Sunday dinner along a riverbank gets the whole family into the act, including the dogs.

Above: Edouard Manet's *Déjeuner sur l'Herbe* probably is the world's most famous work of art on the subject of picnics. With great flair, the French found solutions to a hot summer afternoon.

Right: Could it be that the picnickers in this vintage photograph are indulging in our King Cake on page 37? After all, the tradition we've adapted to a picnic for Mardi Gras has been around since the Middle Ages.

Putting the Food Together

In the ideal picnic, there is fun for all participants, including the cook. To keep preparations simple, bakeries and delicatessens should play a big part in the plans. Most of the recipes in **The Complete Book of Picnics** are simple as well as savory, and the food can be prepared easily at home ahead of time. A few of the recipes are challenging but worth the extra effort for a special occasion.

Because picnics are a national pastime, many of these recipes are all-American with a strong regional accent, such as the **Southern Angel Biscuits** on page 31. Others follow an international theme; see **Philippine Lumpia** on page 61 or Russian Easter cake on page 56. Traditional dishes have also been adapted for picnicking. **Pumpkin Soup** on page 35 is an example.

Since everyone sticks to favorite recipes when it comes to potato salad, deviled eggs and similar dishes, we leave it to you when our menus call for these traditional choices. The picnics presented usually have complete menus, but don't hesitate to take something from one and combine with others to create your own. Also, check the **Instant Picnics** chart on page 89 for no-work, fast get-aways.

Collecting for a Picnic

Before we photographed each picnic for this book we collected dishes, baskets and tablecloths from friends and staff members as well as specialty shops to create the atmosphere or theme we wanted. Let these photos suggest items that you have never before considered for picnicking, such as a shiny red wagon for a rolling buffet. Use things you already have as well as others that can be borrowed. More than any other form of entertaining, picnics, especially big ones, seem made for lending and borrowing.

We feel that every picnic should start with a basket or carrier so we used a wide variety — from a classic English hamper fitted with china and crystal to Japanese stacked lacquer lunch trays; from the familiar open top woven basket to a string shopping bag. There is a chapter about baskets and other equipment that can make it all easier, plus some do-it-yourself totes and tables.

In **The Complete Book of Picnics** you will find practical suggestions for shopping, packing, transporting, preserving and serving your moveable feasts. There are checklists of items to keep in your larder for fast get-aways and a source directory for ready-made foods.

To sum up, picnics are portable feasts bringing together food, friends and fun. Mole, in Kenneth Grahame's classic **Wind In The Willows**, speaks for picnickers everywhere when he confronts an unbelievable array of picnic foods in a sunlit scene.

"'What a day I'm having!' he said. 'Let us start at once!'

"'Hold hard a minute, then!' said the rat . . . . staggering under a fat, wicker luncheon basket . . . .

"'What's inside it?' asked the Mole, wiggling with curiosity.

"'There's cold chicken inside it," replied the Rat briefly; 'coldtonguecoldhamcoldbeefpickledgherkinssaladfrenchrollscresssandwidgespottedmeatgingerbeerlemonadesodawater —'

"'Oh stop, stop,' cried the Mole in ecstasies, 'This is too much!'"

Picnics American Style

The Great American Picnic springs from European foods and cooking techniques introduced by the founding fathers in combination with the rich native harvests and preparation methods of the American Indians. The first Thanksgiving was, after all, a picnic.

Lurking in the history books are descriptions of other memorable early American picnics. Pioneers held one such celebration — a Fourth of July picnic — on the banks of the Platte River under a canopy of tent cloths supported by four wagons. The group reportedly serenaded themselves with "The Star Spangled Banner" and munched on wheat rolls, boiled beans and salt pork, bean broth, bacon, pies, peaches, stewed and dried fruits.

Through the years the possibilities for picnics in America have become as diverse and enticing as the regional cooking created by immigrants from every corner of the globe — French-heritage Creole foods of South Louisiana, Spanish and Mexican influences in the Southwest, the Oriental flavor in California, hearty German-inspired Pennsylvania Dutch farm fare. Such international roots expanded into a vast repertoire featuring the natural produce of our continent — from mouth-watering New England clams to the Deep South mainstay of fried chicken; from smoked salmon Northwest Indian-fashion to tender Iowa corn fresh from the field; wines from the vineyards of New York and California; loaves of pumpernickel and rye from great city delicatessens and homebaked goods from country stores; and all the lush seasonal vegetables and fruits that seem created for picnicking. Include also that original outdoor treat, the watermelon. The fare in this chapter is all-American, but the emphasis is regional.

The following pages offer our ideas for picnicking American Style but add your own variations on the theme: a country outing topped with down-home fare from Pennsylvania farm country, an impromptu spread of Wisconsin cheese and the best of American beers, hot Texas chili or barbecue after a chilly day hike, a breakfast of rainbow trout from the Rocky Mountains. And don't forget the all-American staples, the rib-stickers of a million picnics — sandwiches, hot dogs and hamburgers!

Early American picnics were called "frolics" and consisted of music, games, and flirtations as well as good food. With this in mind, keep **your** American picnics filled with the same ingredients.

Above: July 4th is the major picnic day in the United States. In Washington, D.C., masses of picnickers annually crowd onto The Mall to lunch amidst public monuments.
Opposite: A family celebration in the park features cold roast beef with horseradish sauce, potato salad, pickles, marinated vegetables and, of course, Mom's apple pie, later to be topped off with hand-cranked ice cream. Adding to the Independence Day spirit are flags held aloft by an all-American picnic treat, cold watermelon.

Thanksgiving Dinner

With the unexpected arrival of so many Indians at Plymouth Colony's first harvest celebration in 1621, the only solution for the Pilgrims was to set up tables and eat outdoors. The result was possibly America's earliest picnic and the beginning of a grand tradition of good al fresco eating. If you live where climate permits, stage your own recreation of the first Thanksgiving. Choose an outdoor location that also offers some shelter from the usually unpredictable late November weather.

Unless you have an enormous number of guests and unlimited funds you'll want to simplify the menu of the first Thanksgiving. Chronicles record that the Pilgrim forebears, with thanks to the visiting Wampanoags, gorged on lobsters, mussels or "muskles", clams or "slams," eels, ducks, geese, wild turkeys and venison. Vegetables were limited to pumpkin presented by the Indians and mush made from hard corn.

Plenty of fresh bog cranberries and nuts were gathered from the forests. Preserved wild strawberries, plums and cherries were eaten with hoe cakes and biscuits. The Pilgrims provided barley beer and jugs of new wine from native grapes.

Dessert selection was limited to popcorn balls made with maple syrup and Indian pudding of pounded cornmeal sweetened with molasses.

For our outdoor Thanksgiving we adapt a menu that echoes early colonial life without being totally authentic. You'll probably take the liberty of adding forks, not in common use until some years after the original feast. If you insist on authenticity, feel free to eat with clamshells.

Two weathered patchwork quilts used as covering for a portable metal picnic table add early American atmosphere to an outdoor Thanksgiving dinner. Basket trays are lightweight, easily carried serving pieces for stuffed squash and glazed ducklings. Shells contain smoked seafoods, reminiscent of the harvests of the sea that were so vital to the colonists. Rounds of pumpkin bread baked in coffee tins go perfectly with the hot seafood bisque ladled from a bean pot.

Thanksgiving Dinner for 12

Canned Smoked Clams, Mussels and Oysters

Lobster Bisque

Orange Glazed Roast Ducklings

Baked Corn

Stuffed Acorn Squash

Jellied Cranberry Relish

Biscuits / Spicy Pumpkin Bread

Strawberry Jam / Plum Jelly
Persimmon Pudding with Hard Sauce

Mincemeat Pie
Red and White Jug Wines
Herbal Tea

(Recipe follows)

Lobster Bisque

A rich bisque gives us reason to be thankful for the harvests from the sea — the perfect beginning to the feast day.

- ¾ cup butter or margarine
- 1 cup chopped onion
- 1 cup diced celery
- ¾ cup sliced carrot
- 1 cup dry white wine
- 1 cup fish stock or chicken broth
- ½ cup minced parsley
- 1 bay leaf, crushed
- ¼ teaspoon each thyme and cayenne
- 1 large can (28 oz.) Italian plum tomatoes
- ¼ cup flour
- 3 cups milk, scalded
- 2 pounds cooked lobster meat, diced or finely chopped in food processor
- 1 cup whipping cream, heated
- Salt and pepper to taste
- ¼ cup sherry

1. Melt ½ cup butter in a heavy saucepan and sauté onion, celery and carrot until onion is transparent.

2. Add wine, stock or broth, parsley, bay leaf, thyme, cayenne and tomatoes. Simmer 45 minutes, stirring occasionally, then strain mixture through a fine sieve. Discard vegetables.

3. Melt remaining ¼ cup butter, stir in flour and blend with wire whisk. Scald milk, add all at once and whisk until white sauce is smooth and thickened.

4. Slowly add the strained broth to the white sauce. Stir in lobster meat and simmer for 20 minutes. Do not allow to boil. Turn off heat and add the heated cream. Add salt and pepper to taste; stir in sherry.

Makes 12 small portions.

Note: This bisque can be made with crab, scallops or shrimp, alone or in combination. Make it a day ahead, chill, and reheat just before leaving. Reheat slowly and do not allow to boil. Pour into preheated thermos or wrap soup pot in foil and several layers of newspaper. The soup can also be transported to the picnic chilled and reheated over a barbecue or portable gas stove.

Orange Glazed Roast Ducklings

Allow one 5 to 6-pound domestic duckling for every three persons. Pick and singe, if necessary. Salt the cavities and stuff with quartered onions, apples or celery stalks. Truss openings with skewers and string or needle and thread. Place birds on a rack in a roasting pan and place in oven preheated to 450°F/230°C. Immediately turn heat down to 350°F/180°C. Bake, uncovered, about 15 minutes per pound or until tender; leg should move freely when tested. Do not overcook or the birds will be dry. Prick skin in several places while roasting to drain fat. Spoon excess fat from pan. Pour glaze over ducks about 15 minutes before they are done. Return to oven for completion of cooking.

Orange Glaze: Combine 1 cup orange marmalade or preserves, ½ cup light honey and 2 tablespoons orange flavored liqueur. Blend well over low heat.

Makes glaze for 4 ducklings.

Note: Wrap ducks individually in foil, then in newspapers to keep warm. If the destination is nearby, transport them in the covered baking pan. Or roast a day ahead and serve cold.

Stuffed Acorn Squash

1. Wash 6 small acorn squash, cut each in half lengthwise and scoop out seeds.

2. Fill each cavity with a favorite stuffing mixture or chopped apples and raisins.

3. Place squash in shallow pan and add ¼ inch of water. Bake at 375°F/190°C for about an hour or until squash is tender. Cover with foil toward the end of the cooking period to prevent overbrowning.

Serve ½ squash to each person.

Above: When staging autumn picnics, be sure to select a site that has some type of shelter. Our Thanksgiving dinner in San Francisco's Golden Gate Park was briefly interrupted by a sudden shower just as Charles Deaton began carving. Quick action saved the day as everyone grabbed the table and moved it to the log cabin porch. Serving continued, as shown on the next page.

Below: Table decoration is just as important to the outdoor feast as in the dining room. A pottery bowl overflows to restate the harvest theme. If our biscuit supply appears low it is because one of our young guests decided that cold biscuits slathered with homemade jelly are really all that's needed for a great picnic.

Baked Corn

1. Beat 6 eggs well in mixing bowl. Add 3 tablespoons sugar (or more to taste), 1 teaspoon salt, 6 cups whole kernel corn (fresh, canned, or frozen) and ½ cup melted butter.

2. Mix thoroughly and pour into buttered 12 by 8-inch baking dish.

3. Bake uncovered in 350°F/180°C oven for 30 to 40 minutes or until just firm.

Serves 12.

Spicy Pumpkin Bread

Bake bread several days or even weeks ahead and freeze. Thaw the night before the picnic.

| 2 cups pumpkin (fresh or canned) |
| 2 cups sugar |
| ½ cup butter, melted |
| 3 eggs |
| ½ cup milk |
| 1 cup all-purpose flour |
| 1 cup whole wheat flour |
| 2 teaspoons baking soda |
| 1 tablespoon baking powder |
| 1 teaspoon salt |
| 1½ teaspoon ground cinnamon |
| ½ teaspoon each ground cloves and nutmeg |
| 1 cup each pecans or walnuts and white raisins |

1. Combine pumpkin, sugar, butter, eggs and milk in large mixing bowl.

2. Sift together flours, soda, baking powder, salt and spices. Add to pumpkin mixture and mix just enough to blend ingredients. Stir in nuts, raisins.

3. Spread in three well-greased loaf pans (8 by 4 inches) or pour into three 1-pound greased coffee cans. Bake in 350°F/180°C oven for about 1 hour, or until toothpick inserted near center comes out clean and loaf has slightly pulled away from sides. Cool before slicing. Makes 3 loaves.

Baked Persimmon Pudding

Select persimmons that are fully ripe, almost mushy, for this dark, moist dessert.

| 2 cups all-purpose flour |
| 2 teaspoons baking soda |
| 1 teaspoon salt |
| 2 cups sugar |
| 1 cup seedless raisins |
| 1 cup chopped walnut meats (optional) |
| 2 cups sieved persimmon pulp |
| 2 teaspoons vanilla |
| Hard Sauce (recipe follows) |

1. Sift flour; measure and sift again with soda, salt and sugar into mixing bowl. Add raisins and nuts (optional), stir lightly.

2. Mix in persimmon pulp and vanilla; stir just until dry ingredients are moistened. Pour into a greased and floured 12 by 9-inch baking pan.

3. Set in a shallow pan of hot water. Bake in a moderate oven at 350°F/180°C for 1½ hours, or until golden brown. Serve with small portions of Hard Sauce, or cut fancy shapes from Hard Sauce and decorate pudding.

Serves 12.

Hard Sauce: Sift 1 cup powdered sugar. In small mixing bowl, cream 4 tablespoons softened butter and gradually add sugar. Beat until well blended. Add 1 tablespoon vanilla or brandy. Beat in 2 or 3 tablespoons milk, depending on consistency you desire. Beat until smooth, chill thoroughly.

Makes 1 cup.

Rich, dark persimmon pudding topped with hard sauce is the perfect finale. Whether you are lucky enough to have native American persimmons or use improved Oriental hybrids, home-grown or from the market, be sure the fruit is very ripe and mushy. The dessert can be made a day or two ahead and eaten cold, or baked on Thanksgiving morning and transported while warm, wrapped in foil and insulated with layers of newspaper and a dish towel.

Above: Undaunted by rain, everyone continued serving themselves after moving beneath the cabin shelter. Log seats on the porch were handy for diners with heaped plates. The molded cranberry relish in the foreground was prepared two days in advance and was transported to the site still in its mold.

Alternative Menu Suggestions:

● Instead of canned, consider starting off with fresh oysters or clams on the halfshell.
● Gourmet shops often sell canned seafood bisques, but the price will be high.
● If ducks are unavailable or seem too expensive or troublesome, turkey is always appropriate. To prevent spoilage at picnics it's best to bake stuffing separately instead of inside the bird. If you're lucky enough to have access to wild game such as venison, roast meats also lend the authentic flavor of the first Thanksgiving.
● Although the original feast was low in vegetables and no salads were served, don't hesitate to add your family favorites to the menu.
● Turn to page 101 for a food preparation schedule and tips on transporting.

Vermont Snow Snack

There's probably no more picturesque setting for a winter picnic than the woods of Vermont during sugaring-off time with the smell of boiling maple syrup floating out of the sugar house. Today, as in years past, families in New England love to pour the hot syrup over clean new snow and let it harden into a taffy-textured treat. The traditional accompaniment is sour pickles — definitely an acquired taste!

For an authentic Vermont touch to your picnic, pour maple syrup from the can or hot from a thermos onto fresh snow. This may not produce a stiff maple taffy, but the syrupy snow, stirred with big wooden spoons, is fun to eat. If you plan this winter picnic in regions with no snow, homebaked Maple Cream Cupcakes are a good substitute dessert.

Include a thermos of hearty navy bean soup, an old New England dish that originated as a use for leftover baked beans. This picnic is perfect for a weekend with the kids, an après ski supper or an ice skating party. For that matter, it could become a good excuse for a cold weather gathering anywhere.

Snow Picnic for 4

Navy Bean Soup

Grilled Pork Sausage Links
Baked Stuffed Potatoes

Sour or Dill Pickles
Maple Syrup Snow or
Maple Cream Cupcakes

Coffee / Hot Cocoa

(Recipe follows)

After hearty, hot bean soup and baked potatoes, Cathy and Candy brought out the maple syrup to make maple ice cream in the snow. It took only a couple of stirs of the spoon and a sticky taste to convince young Alissa, skeptical at first. An occasional bite of sour pickle seemed just right, too.

Navy Bean Soup

3 cups baked beans
(leftover or canned)
1 cracked ham hock or
a ham bone, with
some meat
3 cups chicken broth
3 cups water
1 onion, chopped
1 carrot, diced
1 large stalk celery,
chopped
1 small can (8 oz.)
tomatoes, with liquid
3 cloves garlic, minced
Salt and pepper to
taste

1. Combine all ingredients, bring to a boil, reduce heat, cover and simmer slowly for about 3 hours.

2. Remove ham hock and cut meat from the bone. Slice into bite-size pieces and reserve.

3. Purée half the soup in a blender or food processor. Combine with remaining soup, add ham pieces and pour into hot thermos jugs, ready for departure. Or refrigerate overnight and reheat just before packing the picnic.

Makes 4 ample servings.

Baked Stuffed Potatoes

Take along baked potatoes wrapped in foil for reheating over a hibachi at the picnic site while sausages grill.

4 large baking potatoes
¼ cup butter
¼ cup milk
Salt and pepper to
taste
3 ounces Cheddar
cheese, grated
Butter

1. Bake potatoes at 375°F/190°C until tender, about 1½ hours.

2. Remove from oven and when cool enough to handle, carefully cut off tops without breaking the skin. Scoop most of the pulp into a bowl, mash well with butter, milk and seasonings. Stuff potato skins with this mixture, sprinkle with grated cheese and dot with butter. Wrap in foil, reheat over picnic grill.

Serves 4.

Maple Cream Cupcakes

1. Bake cupcakes using a favorite spice cake recipe or package mix.

2. Frost with Maple Cream made by creaming together ¼ cup softened butter or margarine and 2 cups powdered sugar. Gradually beat in ¼ cup maple syrup.

Makes frosting for 24 cupcakes.

New England Clambakes

Consider the temptations of the New England clambake: an all-day beach party culminating in a feast of mouth-watering steamed seafoods and vegetables seasoned with oceans of butter, enjoyed with copious amounts of cold beer or cider, and topped off with icy melon slices. Clambakes originated with the East Coast Indians long before the first European settlers stepped ashore.

Traditional Feasts

For the traditional version, freshly dug clams are first well-scrubbed and then soaked in fresh water while a pit is made and lined with smooth stones. A fire is lighted in the middle of it. Several hours later, when the fire has died down and the stones are sufficiently heated, wet seaweed is quickly piled on the hot rocks. Then clams, lobsters, husked corn, small whole peeled onions, foil-wrapped potatoes, and sometimes quartered chickens are layered in the hot pit. The contents are covered with a wet tarpaulin to allow the food to steam.

The highlight is, of course, when the tarpaulin is removed after about an hour and the contents of the pit rushed to waiting pots of melted butter. This tradition is so time-consuming, however, that nowadays large-scale clambakes are generally produced by professional bake-masters, or only the more adventurous picnickers.

Shortcut Clambakes

Regardless, anyone, anywhere can try a **modified** clambake and the eating pleasures will far outweigh any work you put in to it. Today, with clams and lobsters flown fresh from New England to many states, it's possible to enjoy the clambake experience wherever you are, with or without a beach.

One possible shortcut involves a steel drum set into the earth a few inches for heat insulation. This saves digging a pit and the drum serves as a steamer, with hot stones traditionally lining the bottom. Top stones with fresh wet seaweed, layers of food as outlined above, another layer of seaweed and a tight lid. Steaming by this method should take about an hour. Lift the lid to see if the clams have opened.

Simplest of all, clams can be steamed over a campfire or portable stove in a large pot as in the following recipe. Seaweed, when it's available, can be added to impart an authentic flavor. Rockweed, a seaweed unfortunately unavailable beyond the New England shore, is the best, but wet ferns and leaves can be substituted in beachless areas. (Be sure you know the leaves you use — don't toss in something like poison ivy by mistake.)

Whatever clambake version you choose, be sure to provide an ample supply of napkins or kitchen hand towels, followed by moist towelettes if there's no water nearby for wash-up. When you pack the picnic basket, be sure to include nut or shellfish crackers to break the lobster claws.

The five picnics following our typical New England feast are regional variations on the clambake theme.

Right: Seaweed collected during low tide not only can line a steampot, but also serve as an improvised jump rope for late afternoon fun on the beach. Plan your clambake to be ready to serve in time to watch the sunset as you dine. Hurricane lamps or candles inside glass shades provide light along with the campfire for afterdinner conversation, music and cleanup.

Photographer Dick Rowan and wife Claudia enjoy oceanside dining that's even simplier than the clambake variations described above. A collection of fish and shellfish grilled on a portable hibachi offers great, fresh flavor for minimal effort.

Clambake for 8

Steamed Seafood & Chicken with Vegetables

Boston Baked Beans

Melted Butter

Brown Bread

Tomato Relish

Beer / Cold Cider / Hot Coffee

Chilled Melon Slices

(Recipe follows)

Choosing Seafood

In selecting ingredients for your clambake, purchase everything as close to cooking time as possible. In choosing **clams**, the smaller they are, the better. Those beyond 3 inches across are bound to be tough, less succulent and should be avoided.

Whether you dig your own or buy from a seafood merchant, choose only clams that are tightly closed. The clam should show life by moving slightly when you touch an object to the "neck" at the corner of the shell. Those with opened shells or limp necks hanging out definitely should be passed up, and any clams that fail to open during the cooking process should also be discarded.

If clams are served with other seafood, plan on about 10 per guest. When served alone, allow at least 2 dozen per serving.

Mussels should be as fresh as possible and never eaten uncooked. Pick up a mussel and try to move the two shells back and forth. If the shells slide, chances are they're filled with mud, not mussels,

and should be discarded. Clean mussels by scraping off barnacles to remove sand and clipping beards. Cook as you would clams. Discard any mussels with closed shells after cooking. Allow about 1 quart per serving.

Lobsters should be purchased alive and kicking. Tails when stretched out flat should spring back into their familiar curl. Ideal weight is from 1¼ to 2½ pounds. Larger ones will be tough. Serve one half with other seafood to each guest; if you feel extravagant, plan for a whole lobster per person.

Hard-shelled crabs should also appear quite lively when purchased. There isn't much meat on small crabs, so plan on several per person. One large hard-shelled crab serves two.

Keep live lobsters and crabs refrigerated, but not directly on ice and never immersed in water, until cooking time. Rubber bands can hold lobster claws in place around a piece of wood to prevent pinches during handling.

Steamed Seafood and Chicken

Here's all the flavor of the traditional clambake with only a portion of the effort.

Seaweed, fern fronds or leaves
Water (about 1 quart)
8 medium-size potatoes, well-scrubbed and wrapped in foil
8 whole medium onions, peeled, or about 24 pearl onions
2 chickens (3 to 3½ lbs. each), quartered and wrapped in cheesecloth and tied with string
4 to 8 live lobsters or 16 to 24 live soft-shelled crabs
8 ears of corn with husks, or husked and wrapped in foil
80 (approximately) soft-shelled clams or mussels, well scrubbed and previously soaked in water
Melted butter

1. Wash and soak the seaweed or greenery well. Layer several inches in the bottom of a very large canning kettle or steaming pot. Cover with about 1 quart of water and bring to a boil over high heat.

2. Reduce heat and add foil-wrapped potatoes. Cover tightly and cook approximately 15 minutes before topping with onions and chickens. Cover and continue cooking another 15 minutes.

3. Place lobsters or crabs on chicken layer and cook, covered, another 10 minutes. Top with corn, cover and cook for 10 minutes, then add clams or mussels. Cover and cook until the clams or mussels open, about 10 minutes. Don't overcook or the seafood will be tough. Serve with cups of the resulting broth which has been strained and accompany with plenty of melted butter for dipping seafood and vegetables.

Serves 8.

Boston Baked Beans

Transport this flavorful custom to the clambake by wrapping the casserole or bean pot with foil and newspaper, or place the pot in a plastic-lined insulated basket or carry-all as shown on page 106. If beans get cold, warm them over the fire as the seafood steams. The first recipe is traditional, the second is fast and easy.

2 pounds dried small white, Great Northern or pea beans
Water to cover
⅓ cup dark molasses
2 teaspoons dry mustard
¼ cup brown sugar
¼ teaspoon freshly ground pepper
2 teaspoons salt
2 cups boiling water
¼ pound salt pork
1 medium-size onion, peeled
1 medium-size apple, cored

1. Place beans in a large saucepan and cover with water. Bring to a boil, reduce heat and simmer for 30 minutes. Drain beans and rinse well.

2. Place beans in a 3-quart heavy casserole or bean pot. In a bowl combine molasses, mustard, sugar, pepper and salt with boiling water. Add mixture to the beans.

3. Score salt pork and bury in the beans with the onion and apple.

4. Bake 4 hours, covered, at 300°F/150°C, until beans are tender; then uncover and bake an additional 30 minutes.

Serves 8.

Quick Baked Beans

1. In deep 3-quart casserole or bean pot, combine 2 cans (1½ lbs. each) pork and beans, 1 can (1 lb.) red kidney beans, ½ cup dark molasses, 2 small cans (8 oz. each) tomato sauce, ¼ cup brown sugar, 2 tablespoons prepared mustard, salt and pepper to taste, ½ cup finely chopped green pepper, 1 large onion, chopped, ½ cup crisply cooked, chopped bacon.

2. Bake uncovered for 1 hour at 325°F/160°C.

Serves 8.

Brown Bread

By tradition, Boston brown bread may be either steamed or baked. Here's an easy recipe for the baked version.

1 cup all-purpose flour
2 teaspoons baking soda
1 tablespoon sugar
1 teaspoon salt
2 cups graham flour
1 egg
1 tablespoon melted butter or margarine
½ cup dark molasses
1½ cups buttermilk
1 cup seedless raisins

1. Sift together all-purpose flour, baking soda, sugar and salt. Stir in graham flour.

2. Beat in egg, butter, molasses and buttermilk. Fold in raisins.

3. Pour into greased 8 by 4-inch loaf pan and bake at 325°F/160°C for about 2 hours, or until a wooden skewer inserted in center comes out clean. Cool in pan 10 minutes, then turn out on rack to cool completely.

Makes 1 loaf.

Note: To save time you can buy canned brown bread. Thoroughly heated it's a pretty fair substitute for the homemade counterpart.

Hawaiian Luau

Far away from the New England shores, another great American picnic could be described as a sort of tropical clambake. The luau, too, is traditionally held on a beach and the cooking done in a covered pit. The luau, like the clambake, can easily be transplanted to other terrain.

Seafood is the background of the feast — shrimp, fresh tuna, scallops, whole sea bass. But then the menu departs from the New England fish feed by adding sweet tropical fruits and flavors — bananas, mangoes, coconuts, pineapples and sweet potatoes. Although the expected feature of most luaus is a whole roast suckling pig, smaller cuts of pork also can be succulently roasted or barbecued.

Lavish the luau table — and your guests — with a profusion of fresh flowers. Lighted candles and gardenias or plumeria floating in bowls impart a romantic tropical atmosphere under the stars on a warm night. Invite guests to wear Hawaiian shirts and muumuus. And by all means, laden each guest with flower leis. Simple, white marguerite leis stay fresh and are easy to make and refrigerate the day before the luau.

Our scaled-down luau is a snap to prepare, transport and serve.

Above: Feel free to scale down this luau menu and recipes for an outing with fewer people. Pack supplies into a canvas tote and head to the beach or any pretty outdoor spot close at hand. Simple flower leis, made by stringing daisies or carnations on heavy thread, help put you in the mood. Use a sharp long needle to thread through the thick bases. Anthurium blossoms and a leaf or two pruned from tropical houseplants set the stage, too.

In Hawaii and Tahiti, many hotels feature traditional luaus and native entertainment for guests. On the mainland, simulate your own version to be as simple or elaborate as you wish. Underneath the covering of leaves in this photo, a succulent pig roasts in the pit much like the seafood in New England clambakes. Luau pork usually is served with a variety of fresh fish from the sea, tropical fruits and poi, a cooked and kneaded paste made from taro roots. Also important to a luau are music and dancing.

Glazed Chicken Wings

Prepare this sweet and pungent dish up to three days before the picnic.

- **1 cup soy sauce**
- **1 cup hoisin sauce (available in Oriental or gourmet markets)**
- **½ cup Chinese plum sauce (from same sources)**
- **¾ cup rice or white vinegar**
- **1 cup dry sherry**
- **¼ cup honey**
- **4 cloves garlic, minced**
- **4 dozen chicken wings (about 4 lbs.)**

1. Combine all ingredients except chicken wings and bring to a boil. Simmer 5 minutes, then allow to cool as you prepare wings.

2. Cut off wing tips and reserve for another use (they can be frozen to make broth at a later date). Cut wings at joint, placing pieces in a large glass or plastic container. Pour sauce over and cover tightly. Refrigerate for at least 12 hours, stirring or turning 2 to 3 times to coat evenly.

3. Drain wings and place them in 2 or 3 greased shallow roasting pans (about 13 by 8 inches). Bake, uncovered, turning and basting with remaining sauce every 15 minutes at 375°F/190°C for an hour or until tender.

Serves 12.

Skewered Shrimp and Scallops

Place skewered seafood in marinade before leaving for the luau. At the site, grill on portable hibachi or picnic grounds barbecue.

- **3 pounds large shrimp or prawns, shelled and deveined**
- **3 pounds scallops, cut into bite-size pieces, if large**
- **1 bottle (about 20 oz.) teriyaki sauce (available from gourmet or Oriental markets)**
- **½ cup butter or margarine, melted**
- **Juice of 1 lemon**

1. Thread seafood on 12 skewers and cover with teriyaki sauce for at least 1 hour. Drain, then brush with butter and lemon juice mixture.

2. Grill 4 inches above glowing coals, turning several times, for about 10 minutes.

Serves 12.

Rice Salad

- **6 cups cold cooked rice**
- **1½ cups chopped ripe olives**
- **1 cup (4 jars, 2 oz. each) chopped pimento**
- **1 cup chopped onion**
- **¼ to ½ cup capers, to taste**

1. Combine salad ingredients, reserving some pimentos and capers for garnish.

2. Pour dressing (recipe follows) over salad and toss thoroughly. Garnish with reserved capers and pimentos.

Serves 12.

Dressing: Mix together the following: ½ cup each vinegar and salad oil, 2 teaspoons dry mustard, 1 teaspoon sugar, salt and freshly ground pepper. Shake to blend well.

Tropical Fruit Compote

Vary the fruits with abandon according to personal taste and availability.

- **1 large fresh pineapple**
- **1 mango**
- **1 papaya**
- **2 to 3 bananas**
- **1 cup seedless grapes, halved**
- **¾ cup grated coconut**
- **2 tablespoons grated fresh ginger**
- **½ cup orange flavored liqueur (optional)**
- **Juice of 1 lemon**

1. Peel pineapple and remove core. Peel and seed mango and papaya; peel bananas. Cut all fruit into bite-size pieces.

2. Mix cut fruit and grape halves with the coconut and ginger. Stir in liqueur, lemon juice and chill.

Serves 12.

Note: Take chilled compote to the luau in a cooler. If it is not to be served soon after preparation, peel, slice and add bananas at picnic site.

Lenny's Coconut-Pineapple Drink

This is a delicious, chilly concoction to transport in thermoses. To add atmosphere, consider serving from hollowed pineapple or coconut shells.

- **¾ cup cream of coconut (from gourmet grocery or liquor stores)**
- **1½ cups each milk and pineapple juice**
- **2 bananas**
- **½ cup each banana liqueur and light rum (optional)**

Combine all ingredients in a blender and liquify for several seconds. Serve well chilled over a little crushed ice.

Makes 5 cups to serve 3. (Prepare 4 batches to serve 12. Most blenders have a 5 or 6 cup capacity.)

Tropical Juice: Often "natural foods" stores stock quart bottles of coconut-pineapple drink in their refrigerators. It's good as is or combined with 1 puréed banana, ¼ cup each banana liqueur and rum for each quart of juice.

One quart makes 6 small servings.

Native helpers at an island luau busily prepared coconuts and plantains, tropical fruits resembling firm, green bananas. Papayas, mangoes, passion fruit and pineapples may be added. Tropical fruit usually is available in supermarkets or stores that specialize in Oriental or South American foods. Large leaves are used as serving dishes.

Abalone Steak Picnic

A western variation on the theme of East Coast clambakes involves an adventurous hunt for Pacific abalone climaxing with this sumptuous shellfish sautéed right on the beach.

If you are lucky enough to harvest your own feast, be sure to check up-to-date fishing regulations as to quantity allowed and other restrictions. California law forbids opening abalone on the beach, so you'll have to take them to an adjacent area for cleaning and pounding, a necessity to make them edible.

Fresh abalone steaks are available in many California markets, but the state does not allow the scarce, expensive fish to be shipped to other areas. However, canned and frozen abalone from Mexico and Japan are widely available. They're ready to cook — and the shelling and pounding already done for you.

Fresh abalone is removed from the shell by running a knife between the meat and the shell. After the dark portion is trimmed and discarded, the edible part must be tenderized by pounding with a heavy mallet on a flat hard surface until the meat is limp. Slice into very thin steaks cutting across the grain with a sharp knife. Sauté over a campfire, on a hibachi or portable stove.

To fully appreciate the delicacy of sautéed abalone, serve with only a green salad, good crusty bread, fresh seasonal fruits, and beer, chilled white wine or sparkling mineral water.

Abalone Picnic for 8
Sautéed Abalone Steaks

Tossed Green Salad

French Bread and Sweet Butter

Seasonal Fruit

White Wine / Mineral Water / Beer

(Recipe follows)

After the divers have taken the rock-clinging abalones from the sea, the shellfish are opened and prepared in a nearby area. The meat is removed from the opalescent shell by running a knife between the muscle and the shell. Next, abalone gets a not-so-gentle pounding to tenderize the meat. Finally, it is sliced into thin steaks for sautéeing.

Sautéed Abalone Steaks

Serve directly from the sauté pan decorated with a collar of lettuce or a sprinkling of minced parsley for color.

| 1 cup all-purpose flour |
| 1 teaspoon salt |
| ¼ teaspoon freshly ground pepper |
| 2 eggs |
| 2 tablespoons milk |
| 1 cup fine dry bread or cracker crumbs, or cornmeal |
| 1 teaspoon minced fresh herbs or ½ teaspoon dried herbs (basil, chervil and tarragon) |
| 8 abalone steaks, pounded |
| Butter or salad oil for cooking |

1. Combine flour, salt and pepper in a shallow bowl. In a separate bowl, quickly beat eggs and milk. In a third bowl combine the crumbs or cornmeal and herbs.

2. With paper towels pat the steaks dry; dip into seasoned flour. Shake gently to remove excess. Dip into the egg mixture, roll in the crumbs. Make sure crumbs adhere to all surfaces; pat off excess.

3. Sauté in a small amount of butter or oil for about 2 minutes per side or until lightly golden.

Serves 8.

Note: Many cooks prefer abalone without the breading. Simply salt and pepper to taste and dust lightly with flour before cooking.

The Pacific provides a dramatic panorama for outdoor dining. The abalone steaks are served directly from the pan in which they were sautéed over a campfire. A band of lettuce adds color. Homebaked bread, a tossed green salad and fresh seasonal fruits complete the menu.

Louisiana Fish Fry

Major portions of this picnic must be cooked on the site and served while piping hot. That's part of the fun — nothing can match the aroma of fresh fish frying outdoors. What a great picnic to end a day of fishing, boating or hiking!

We've chosen a Louisiana favorite combination, catfish and hush puppies, but you can adapt the idea to any local fish, the fresher the better. Just to be on the safe side, in case your catch is skimpy, make a stop at the local fish market and stash enough for dinner in an ice chest.

The tranquility of Black River Lake, Louisiana, in the background and the Spanish moss canopy over the picnic table makes just-fried catfish and hush puppies taste even better. Tin cups and pie plates, picnic traditions, are easy to carry. Lucille, left, brought along her lemon tarts and James, center, fried the fish over a portable gas cooker. Christine provided the laughs.

Fish Fry for 4

Fried Catfish

Hush Puppies

French-Fried Potatoes

Salad Plate: Lettuce Leaves

Sliced Tomatoes

Sweet Onion Rings

Mother's Lemon Tarts

Cold Soft Drinks

Hot Coffee

(Recipe follows)

Fried Catfish

Both fresh and frozen catfish are now available in markets across the country. But if you can't find them, substitute any firm-fleshed fish.

1. Season a cleaned whole small fish or fillets of larger fish with salt and pepper. Coat the fish with fine cornmeal or packaged fish-fry coating by shaking the fish in a bag containing some of the meal. Pour salad oil into a deep heavy frying pan to a depth of 1½ to 2 inches. Heat to 375°F/ 190°C on a thermometer or until a small cube of bread browns well in about 60 seconds.

2. Add fish one at a time, avoiding overcrowding. Adjust fire so that fish cook in about 20 min-utes, or until golden brown. The fish should float on the hot oil. Drain on paper towels. Cover loosely with foil to keep warm while potatoes and hush puppies cook. Serve with fresh lemon wedges.

Allow at least 1 small catfish per person.

Hush Puppies

American lore has it that this dish came about as bits of batter were cooked and thrown to satisfy hungry dogs while the smell of fish frying filled the air. Throughout the South they've become time-honored companions to catfish. Hush puppies fry quickly in the same pan, right after the french fries are done and removed to a platter.

1½ cups yellow cornmeal	
¾ cup flour	
4 teaspoons baking powder	
¾ teaspoon salt	
2 eggs	
¾ cup milk	
¼ cup minced onion	
Oil for deep frying	

1. Sift dry ingredients together. Beat eggs and combine with milk. Stir in dry ingredients, add onions and let stand for about 15 minutes.

2. Drop by tablespoon-fuls in deep hot fat (375°F/ 190°C) and cook quickly until golden brown, about 2 minutes. Drain on paper towels. Serve hot.

Makes about 18 two-inch hush puppies.

Mother's Lemon Tarts

These lemon tarts are lighter and more delicate than most — a perfect ending to any fish fry.

2½ tablespoons corn-starch	
¾ cup sugar	
¼ teaspoon salt	
1 cup boiling water	
1 tablespoon butter or margarine	
2 egg yolks, well beaten	
¼ cup freshly squeezed lemon juice	
1 teaspoon grated lemon rind	
6 baked 3-inch tart shells (use your own pastry recipe or packaged or frozen shells)	
Whipped cream (optional) or Meringue (recipe follows)	

1. Combine cornstarch, sugar and salt in top of double boiler. Gradually add boiling water to the mixture and cook over hot water at medium heat until thickened, stirring constantly to prevent lumps. Cook and stir 5 minutes longer. Mix in butter.

2. Pour a little of the slightly cooled mixture into the beaten egg yolks and blend well. Combine egg mixture with the remaining hot cornstarch mixture. Add lemon juice and rind and cook 1 minute. Pour into baked tart shells or 9-inch pie crust. Serve plain, with meringue, or top with a dollop of whipped cream when cool.

Makes 6 tarts.

Meringue: Beat 2 egg whites with ¼ teaspoon cream of tartar until stiff but not dry. Beat in 4 to 5 tablespoons sugar a little at a time until meringue is thick and shiny. Spread on tarts or pie and brown in a 350°F/180°C oven for about 10 minutes, until lightly tinged with brown.

San Francisco Crab Lunch

San Franciscans enjoy a six-month feast that runs from December through May — the length of Dungeness crab season. These large, succulent-fleshed, hard-shell crabs are found along the Pacific Coast from Alaska down to California's Monterey Peninsula.

A large, cracked crab with homemade mayonnaise accompanied by a leafy green salad, a loaf of famous San Francisco sourdough or other good French bread, chilled white wine and perhaps a chocolate truffle or two from a special pastry shop are all that's needed for a quickly prepared, sumptuous lunch on a grassy hillside.

During the season, fresh crab is widely available in western fish markets. You can buy them cooked, cleaned and cracked. When fresh crab isn't available, you can make do with frozen king crab legs from Alaska or flaked canned crab meat tossed in a salad.

Note: Carry cooked crabs in several layers of newspaper. Don't forget plastic bags for the shells at clean-up time.

Cracked Crab Lunch
Cracked Crab with Homemade Mayonnaise
Leafy Salad
Sourdough Bread
Chocolate Truffles
White Wine

While lunching on cracked Dungeness crab, these picnickers can enjoy the multi-layered vista of San Francisco, both old and new. This row of Victorian houses predates the 1906 earthquake and fire. Adjacent to hilly Alamo Square, the row contrasts with the modern downtown skyline. And beyond, the Oakland hills are visible across the Bay. Visitors can pick up cooked crab at markets along Fisherman's Wharf. Readily available, the unique sourdough bread, a good California white wine and fruit juice for the kids rounds out an easy tourists' picnic. Follow the same idea wherever you travel, buying whatever foods are regional. Then find a spot where you can enjoy local scenery.

Crayfish Boil

Freshwater crayfish (called crawfish or crawdads in some places) are found on every continent except Africa. The streams of America abound with the tiny crustaceans; recently they have been raised commercially. Resembling miniature lobsters, crayfish are the ubiquitous **garni** in French **nouvelle cuisine,** popular fare from the California delta country, the bayous of the South, the streams of the Midwest and prized by gourmets everywhere. They're served in all sorts of fancy dishes, but are at their sweetest, most delicious best when boiled right after they are caught and eaten from their shells.

About catching them: it's almost as easy as the old song directs, "You get a line, I'll get a pole and we'll go down to that crawdad hole." To that information add a small piece of bacon tied to the line and plan to catch crayfish in the wilds from early summer to early autumn.

After catching them, keep live crayfish refrigerated in cool fresh water until cooking time. Provide plenty of oxygen by changing the water frequently. Some European chefs suggest combining the water with nonfat dry milk and keeping the crayfish in it for at least 12 hours to clean out the intestine. Most Americans do not bother, for crayfish can be cleaned after cooking by simply grasping the middle tail fin, giving a firm twist and pulling to remove stomach and intestinal vein.

Handle live crayfish with care to avoid being pinched. Pick up by placing your thumb and first finger over the back and grasping behind the claws.

Boiled Crayfish

1. To cook, drop the live crayfish into boiling salted water. (Or make a court bouillon spiced with 1 tablespoon dried parsley, 1 teaspoon each thyme and marjoram, 1 bay leaf, ½ teaspoon whole black peppers for 4 quarts water.) When the water returns to simmer, cook approximately 2 minutes for tiny, inch-long crayfish, or up to 15 minutes for very large, 6-inch varieties. Overcooking causes meat to toughen.

2. Drain and rinse with cold water to halt cooking process. Meat is tenderest if allowed to rest a few minutes before serving. Serve while still warm, mounded in bowls with melted butter for dipping, or, best of all, thoroughly chilled. Seafood cocktail sauce can be served with chilled crayfish.

Note: To eat crayfish, pull tail from body with fingers. Crack tail between thumbs and fingers of both hands by bending backwards. Pull out meat. If you wish, crack the tiny claws between your teeth and suck out the bits of sweet meat. Allow plenty of crayfish per person. It normally takes 20 crayfish about 4 to 5 inches long to equal the meat of 1 small lobster.

Crayfish are often available in markets, or see source listed on page 93.

Crayfish Boil

Boiled Crayfish

Lettuce, Green Pepper, Onion Rings Salad

Crusty Bread

Lemon Cupcakes

Cold Soft Drinks / Coffee

(Recipe above)

In New Orleans we purchased cooked crayfish-to-go from a French Market cafe and headed to the nearby Mississippi levee to watch modern freighters and old steamboats travel the hazy river. Often there is music from a steam calliope to contribute to the feeling of a Mark Twain lazy afternoon. The chilled freshwater shellfish delicacy is excellent with spicy cocktail sauce, crackers and local beer.

Indian Summer Brunch

Chilled Cucumber Soup

Prepare this easy soup a day ahead and chill overnight in the refrigerator. Pour the cold soup into a thermos and it's ready to go.

- **1 large cucumber (approximately ½ lb.)**
- **¼ cup finely chopped onion**
- **2 tablespoons butter or margarine**
- **1 tablespoon salad oil**
- **2 cups chicken broth**
- **½ teaspoon white wine vinegar**
- **½ teaspoon fresh dill, minced (or ¼ teaspoon dried dill weed)**
- **¼ cup heavy cream (or sour cream)**
- **Salt and pepper to taste**

1. Peel cucumber, slice thinly and set aside.

2. Sauté the onion in butter and oil until tender. Add cucumber, broth, vinegar and dill. Simmer, uncovered, for about 30 minutes.

3. Purée in a blender or food processor. Stir in cream, add salt and pepper to taste and chill.

Serves 2.

Blueberry-Maize Muffins

In these muffins cornmeal is teamed with wild blueberries, also native American. They freeze well and can be kept on hand for quick getaway picnics.

- **1 cup stone ground cornmeal**
- **1 cup whole wheat flour**
- **⅓ cup sugar**
- **4 teaspoons baking powder**
- **½ teaspoon salt**
- **1 egg**
- **1 cup milk**
- **¼ cup melted butter or salad oil**
- **Grated rind of one lemon**
- **1 cup blueberries (fresh or well-drained canned or frozen and thawed)**

1. Combine cornmeal, flour, sugar, baking powder and salt. Mix well.

2. Add egg, milk, butter or oil and lemon rind. Stir just enough to blend. Lightly fold in blueberries to avoid releasing juices.

3. Fill greased muffin pans two-thirds full and bake in a 400°F/205°C oven for about 20 minutes or until lightly browned.

Makes about 15 large muffins.

In autumn, with the summer crowds finally gone, our national and states parks are quiet places to picnic. Designers Craig Bergquist and Christine Dunham took along an Indian rug for streamside relaxing after a Sunday morning stroll through Samuel P. Taylor State Park in northern California.

Select a beautiful morning in Indian summer and head to the forest with your favorite person. Find a quiet stream and spread out a simple brunch on the rocks. Our menu is inspired by the foods of the first Americans who introduced us to smoked fish and corn. Perhaps you'll be lucky enough to find edible berries and watercress growing nearby, but just to play it safe, take along a supply from the supermarket.

Pot Luck Picnicking

Originally the word "picnic" was used to describe a festive occasion when each person in attendance contributed a dish to the meal. All guests shared whatever each pot contained — thus, "pot luck." Such events have been a part of the American scene since our first social get-together. Here we offer photographic evidence that the spirit of pot luck is still very much alive.

"Dinner-on-the-Ground" at the First Baptist Church of Jonesville, Louisiana, for instance, proves that the time-honored custom remains an integral part of both church fellowship and community social life. It all began when families came by horse and buggy for long-lasting revival meetings and church services that prevented members from returning home in time for dinner. Each family brought along its Sunday meal and the entire congregation would share the vast array of food, either spread on the ground or on long tables outdoors.

Today's church dinners are reserved for special days and are probably more sophisticated, but the foods are just as varied and tasty as in bygone times. Anyone who's ever eaten his way through an assortment of family favorites heaped on miles of church dinner tables can testify that this authentic American custom of pot luck provides some of the best eating in the world.

Pioneer families in America often helped each other with building projects such as barn raising. When families and friends got together to work, they provided hearty, transportable foods. At the end, or in the middle of the day's cooperative project, the pot luck picnic was spread.

Nowadays, when friends get together to help a neighbor with a special project, the picnic meal is the highlight of the day. As in the case of a deck raising, the host often furnishes the meat, such as roast turkey, and guests bring along everything else. You might wish to adapt the idea to a spring garden planting afternoon, a house painting picnic, community cleanup, a long day of political campaign activities, or even a wedding.

On a windy, warm autumn morning a hundred friends gathered on the top of Mt. Tamalpais in Marin County, California, to celebrate

Below: Yards and yards of tables loaded with family favorites are shared by members of the congregation at the First Baptist Church in Jonesville, Louisiana. Georgia Taliaferro, left, brought her frothy, cloudlike dessert of oranges and cream, as she has done for many years. The lady in red is Eula Cain, originator of the pecan pie recipe on page 31.

a wedding. The private ceremony had been performed several weeks earlier, but the newlyweds wanted to picnic atop the mountain and to share their joy with friends and family members.

A dozen colorful banners on bamboo poles flagged the site for those unfamiliar with the location. As they arrived, guests were served hot coffee, chilled champagne and orange juice. After a simple ring ceremony at the summit, a promontory with miles of views, everyone joined in the feasting.

This picnic illustrates organized pot luck at its best. Lightweight tables were unfolded and spread with ivory colored patchwork cloths. Picnic baskets held silverware and kept napkins from escaping in the wind. Some guests brought blankets to sit on amongst the trees and dozens of potted yellow and bronze chrysanthemums. The clean-up was a preplanned chore, too, and was accomplished in a matter of minutes.

The newlyweds supplied the champagne, meats and, of course, the wedding cake. Guests were requested to bring specific courses to complete the feast. The final choice of particular dishes was up to each good cook, but a few phone calls assured everyone of a balanced banquet and delicious variety.

Note: See page 101 for ideas for organizing and staging large picnics.

Above: Following a mountaintop wedding ceremony guests moved on to the picnic tables heaped with favorites that everyone brought to this pot luck party. Colorful cotton pennants fluttered from bamboo poles to mark the site. (See page 108.)

The wedding cake, featured a bouquet of autumn flowers that repeated the colors of the potted chrysanthemums massed around nearby tree trunks. Be sure to get official permission well in advance if you plan to stage a large picnic on public grounds.

Midwest Corn Feed

If there's anything even more American than Mom's apple pie, it's corn on the cob. Although the early corn introduced to the settlers by the Indians was a poor, tough and small relative of the plump ears we know today, it became an absolute staple of the pioneer diet. The rich years of farming experience have improved corn to a point where it would barely be recognized by those early Americans.

The height of corn-eating enjoyment is to have a pot of water boiling just a few steps away from the corn field: quickly pick and husk a few ears, pop them into the boiling water for a few moments, douse them with butter and seasonings and dig in.

When summer corn reaches its peak of tender sweetness, invite a group of friends to a feast set up in the vegetable garden, or on the adjacent lawn. Our menu is planned to feature many of the other harvests of the garden, too. Start, as guests gather, with just-picked sliced sweet peppers served with chunks of mild cheese. The meal ends with melons, sweet and juicy off the vine, chilled in tubs of chipped ice. If you wish to add meat to this vegetarian fare, grill some cornfed beef from America's heartland.

Nothing could be easier for the hosts. All that's necessary to prepare beforehand is the vegetable main dish, herbed butter and homemade bread. The rest can be done on site with guests helping; let them pick their own corn and add it to the pot.

If you have no access to a vegetable garden, don't despair. You can still put on a feed that no one will forget. Buy plenty of corn from a nearby farmer or the market. Select the ears carefully. Husks should be moist and supple, the silk a pale gold, the kernels even and small, pale and firm. Corn should be cooked as soon as possible so the natural sugar doesn't turn to starch. Drenched in butter, salt and pepper, corn can almost be a main course for any picnic.

To enjoy corn at its finest hour, set up a portable charcoal grill right in the garden and bring a canning kettle of water to boil. Guests select corn just off the stalks, pull back the husks and tie into place with a strip of husk. Corn goes into boiling water for a few minutes, then is removed easily by husk handles and rushed to waiting herbed butter.

Corn Feed for 10

Sweet Peppers with Cheese Chunks

Vegetable Medley Casserole

Corn on the Cob with Herbed Butter

Tomato Basil Vinaigrette

Whole Wheat Bread / Sweet Butter

Wine Cooler

Assorted Melon Slices or

Apple Pie

(Recipe follows)

Vegetable Medley Casserole

Freely add to this basic recipe whatever garden vegetables are on hand.

½ cup oil	
2 eggplants, unpeeled, cut into small cubes	
2 onions, chopped	
3 cloves garlic, minced	
3 to 4 zucchini, sliced	
½ pound mushrooms, sliced	
6 tomatoes, peeled and chopped	
2 teaspoons each basil and oregano	
Salt and freshly ground pepper to taste	
5 eggs, well beaten	
2 cups mixed grated or shredded melting cheeses (jack, Parmesan, mozzarella or white Cheddar)	
¾ cup fine bread crumbs	
Paprika	

1. In a very large frying pan or dutch oven heat oil over medium heat and sauté eggplant, onion and garlic until soft. Add zucchini and mushrooms, stirring until mushrooms are soft.

2. Add tomatoes and seasonings. Simmer until liquid has evaporated, stirring often. Remove from heat; cool.

3. Stir eggs and 1 cup of the cheese into the cooled vegetable mixture. Pour half of the mixture into a greased 3-quart casserole (or divide among several smaller ones) and sprinkle half the remaining cheese over. Add the rest of the vegetable mixture and top with remaining cheese. Sprinkle with breadcrumbs and paprika.

4. Bake uncovered in a 375°F/190°C oven for approximately 25 minutes or until top has browned.

Serves 10 to 12.

Corn on the Cob

1. Select tender, young sweet corn. Pull the husks back, leaving them intact at the end of the cob. Tie the husks together with a strip of corn husk. Remove silks and drop ears into rapidly boiling salted water for 3 to 5 minutes.

2. Pull out with the husk handle and season to taste with salt, freshly ground pepper and herbed butter. Allow at least 2 ears per person.

Herbed Butter: To **each** cup of softened butter (sweet or salted, as you prefer), add 4 tablespoons minced fresh herbs (thyme, parsley, basil or oregano) or 4 teaspoons crushed dried herbs. Mix well and refrigerate in covered container at least overnight to fully develop herbal flavor. Serve at garden temperature or melt in a saucepan to pour over the corn.

Serves 10.

Tomato Basil Vinaigrette

Slice garden-fresh ripe tomatoes and sprinkle generously with minced fresh basil. Drizzle with olive oil and vinegar and refrigerate at least an hour to develop flavor.

Wine Cooler

For a refreshing summer beverage simply combine your favorite red or white wine with equal parts sparkling mineral water or club soda over plenty of ice. Add wedges of lemon or lime.

Southwestern Picnic

Authentic chuckwagon fare of the American West usually includes some form of barbecue, chili and beans, hearty biscuits or cornbread, along with available fresh fruits.

When the chuckwagon meets the **cantina** the food gets spicy and piquant. Food of the Southwest is a lively combination of the crops of this productive area and delicious south-of-the-border cooking methods.

This very simple menu features a big salad brimming with the tang of the Southwest. Accompanied with ice cold sangría and seasonal fruits, it's all you need for an easy mobile meal.

In the sense of portable outdoor eating, chuckwagon meals are really picnics that date back to the old West. Today's cowboys of all ages still enjoy the tradition of good hearty chuckwagon foods.

A young Arizona cowboy chooses his midday meal from an array of typical foods including barbecued beef, beef stew, chili and beans, biscuits and green salad. The canvas covering provides shelter from the blazing sun. Freely adapt this idea of your own picnicking plans, adding favorite salads, vegetables and desserts.

Southwest Salad Picnic for 4

Leslie's Taco Salad

Fresh Fruit

Iced Sangría

(Recipe follows)

Leslie's Taco Salad

What could be more Western than a denim tablecloth with bandanas as napkins and plates of granite-wear? With food and setting, this very simple picnic captures the flavor of the Southwest. Our taco salad introduces seasonings from neighboring Mexico. To prevent the salad from wilting prepare ingredients at home and package separately in sealed plastic bags or bowls. Toss with the dressing at the picnic site. Carry along fresh fruit for dessert, or eat the wine-soaked fruits from the sangría.

1 pound lean ground beef
1 package (1¼ oz.) taco seasoning mix
½ cup water
1 head iceberg lettuce broken into bite-size pieces
1 tomato, cut into wedges
1 avocado, peeled and sliced
1 can (16 oz.) kidney beans, drained
1 can (8 oz.) garbanzo beans, drained
½ red onion, halved and thinly sliced
1 bottle (8 oz.) French salad dressing
2 cups grated sharp Cheddar cheese
2 cups tortilla chips, broken into small pieces

1. Crumble ground beef and sauté in its own drippings until brown. Drain and discard fat, then add taco seasoning mix and water. Cook, stirring occasionally, until most of the water is gone. Cool thoroughly.

2. In a salad bowl, mix all ingredients with the cooled ground beef, reserving a few slices of avocado, tomato and whole tortilla chips for garnish.

Serves 4.

Note: Cooked and cooled ground beef may be carried in a plastic container and added with the dressing just before serving at the picnic to preserve crispness of lettuce.

Iced Sangría

This popular drink is from Spain, via Mexico. Mix the day before the picnic and store in refrigerator — chilling enhances the flavor.

1 cup water
½ cup sugar
1 quart dry red wine
1 cup orange juice
½ cup orange flavored liqueur (optional)
1 fresh peach, pitted and sliced, or 1 cup sliced canned peaches
1 orange, thinly sliced
1 lemon or lime, thinly sliced
1 bottle (7 oz.) club soda

1. Combine water and sugar and boil for 5 minutes. Cool.

2. Blend cooled syrup with other ingredients, except club soda. Chill well. Pour into large, wide-mouth thermos jug.

3. Add club soda at picnic and serve over plenty of ice.

Serves 4.

Note: White sangría can be made in the same way by substituting dry white wine for the red.

The most friendly, comfortable way to end a Southwestern picnic is with coffee made over a park barbecue grill or portable stove.

Fried Chicken Picnic

When most of us think of picnic fare, Southern fried chicken ranks near the top of the list. In addition to this great American classic, the Deep South has provided a wide range of unique dishes derived not only from family recipes of wealthy European plantation owners but also from the cooking methods introduced by African slaves, and from vegetables, fruit, grains and fish native to the South.

Chances are you won't have access to a cotton field for a Dixieland picnic, but any outdoor locale can provide the opportunity to try these typical dishes.

Keep your adaptation simple. Transport and serve food from colorful self-sealing plastic containers. All the food can be served cold, although you'll probably want to bake the cornbread, fry the chicken and warm the greens just before leaving home. If you can wait till the end, climax the meal with the cutting of an icy crisp watermelon, kept cold in a portable cooler.

Fried Chicken Picnic for 4
Southern Fried Chicken

Turnip Greens / Louisiana Pepper Sauce

Fried Okra / Pickled Okra

Blackeye Pea Salad

Cornbread Sticks

Matilda's Sweet Potato Pie

Soft Drinks

Cold Watermelon

(Recipe follows)

Lee LaRavia's full attention is on his mother as she cuts into an icy cold watermelon. It's an welcome addition to a family meal alongside his dad's field of snowy cotton, and it's Lee's favorite part of the menu. It seems an appropriate occasion to use the ever-popular checked tablecloth. Paper plates, napkins and plastic flatware mean no dishwashing back home. Okra, a favorite vegetable in the South, is offered in two forms: crisp-fried and pickled. The taste is totally different when pickled. Carry in a small ice chest so the pods will be crisp and cold. Louisiana pepper sauce is poured over the turnip greens. Our original salad uses the ubiquitous blackeye pea of the South in an unusual way. Prepare the salad a day in advance to develop the flavor. All these foods can be carried in plastic sealable containers.

Southern Fried Chicken

Fried chicken is probably the most famous and dearly loved American picnic fare. It originated on the plantations, where black cooks would cut plump farm-fresh chickens into serving pieces, bathe them in water or milk, season with salt, plenty of pepper and secret family blends of herbs and spices, roll them in flour and fry in sizzling lard. Hot, the chicken was accompanied by creamy gravy and buttered biscuits. Cold, it still provides the perfect picnic staple.

Today all Southern cooks have their own way of frying chicken — spicy, soft, crisp, with batter or plain. The author's personal favorite is his grandmother Olivia Bell Keith's version.

1. Wash and dry 1 large frying chicken. Cut into serving pieces; season with salt and pepper.

2. Coat generously with flour and place in hot deep salad oil until lightly browned.

3. Reduce heat to low and continue cooking slowly until done, but still juicy inside and golden brown on the outside. Normally this takes about 20 minutes.

Serves 4.

Note: If you prefer a softer outside, place the golden browned chicken in a pan and cover tightly with foil. Bake in a 275°F/ 135°C oven 30 minutes.

Fried Okra

1. The traditional method calls for coating 1 pound thinly sliced okra in ⅓ cup cornmeal.

2. Fry in ½ cup hot oil until golden brown and crisp. Drain on paper towel and sprinkle with salt.

Serves 4.

Louisiana Pickled Okra: See the Ortho book, **All About Pickling**, page 45. Pickled okra is also available commercially packed in many food shops.

Turnip Greens

1. Wash 3 bunches (1 lb. each) of fresh greens several times to remove all dirt.

2. Place in large pot with water that clings to the leaves from the final rinse.

3. Add about ½ pound of bacon slices or salt pork, a chopped onion (optional) and salt and pepper to taste.

4. Cook over low heat until greens and pork are tender, about an hour.

At the picnic be sure to dip cornbread sticks (made from your favorite recipe or a packaged mix) into the "pot likker" or liquid from the greens. Let each picnicker add bottled Louisiana pepper sauce to taste.

Serves 4.

Blackeye Pea Salad

Here's an unusual way to serve another Southern staple.

1. Cook 1 pound shelled fresh blackeye peas gently in 1 cup salted water (with a piece of salt pork, if desired) until peas are just tender, but still hold shape, about 30 minutes.

2. Drain and mix while hot with the following Vinaigrette Dressing.

3. Chill overnight, then stir in ¼ cup each chopped parsley and onion.

Serves 4.

Vinaigrette Dressing: Combine ⅓ cup salad oil ¼ cup vinegar, ⅛ teaspoon each dry mustard, sugar and tarragon, 1 small clove garlic, finely minced, and salt and pepper to taste.

Makes ½ cup.

Southern cooks gave us a perennial picnic favorite—fried chicken. For still-warm flavor and aroma, fry the chicken just before leaving home, wrap in foil and insulate with newspapers and a dishtowel. Most everyone also enjoys it cold, in which case the chicken can be fried the day before. When you're in a hurry or have a last minute picnic rush, chicken from a fast food chain makes an acceptable substitute.

Matilda's Sweet Potato Pie

In the South this pie is often eaten along with the meat course, but obviously can be served as dessert.

4 medium-size sweet potatoes, about 2 pounds
½ cup butter or margarine, softened
2 cups sugar
4 eggs
1 teaspoon cinnamon
½ teaspoon ground cloves
1 teaspoon vanilla
1 cup buttermilk
½ teaspoon baking soda (added to buttermilk)
2 unbaked 9-inch pastry shells or 12 three-inch tart shells
Whipping cream (optional)

1. Peel potatoes, cut into quarters and cook in slightly salted water until tender, about 15 minutes. Whirl in blender, food processor or mixer until smooth.

2. Add remaining ingredients (except pastry) and pour into pastry shells. Bake at 375°F/ 190°C for approximately 40 minutes or until top just begins to brown and feels firm to the touch. For dessert, serve warm or cold with a dollop of sweetened whipped cream.

Serves 12.

Note: This pie freezes very successfully. Carry it freshly baked or thawed, fitted snugly into a box, plastic carrier, or on the special rack for pies in some picnic baskets.

Sweet potato pie is a Southern classic that is delicious eaten along with the meat course; it also makes a marvelous dessert. Our recipe from Matilda Adams is one of the best.

Plantation Buffet

Plantation Buffet for 10
Smoked Ham with Orange Glaze

Candied Yams
Melon Basket:

Chilled Cantaloupe, Honeydew and
Watermelon Balls
Angel Biscuits / Fig Preserves

Pecan Pie

Pineapple-Strawberry Torte

Minted Iced Tea.

(Recipe follows)

Magnificent moss-draped oak trees frame the antebellum Devereaux mansion in Natchez, Mississippi, setting for an updated version of heritage elegance and formality. For our buffet on a hot summer afternoon, today's young Scarlett O'Haras and Rhett Butlers gathered around foods that have made Southern cookery legendary.

In the middle of the sun-drenched grassy lawn, a folding picnic table gleamed with white linen overlaid with antique lace. Sterling silver and crystal serving pieces, along with handpainted heirloom plates, rounded out the traditional setting. After serving themselves from the buffet, the young picnickers settled down to eat on the spacious lawn among the cut magnolia blossoms and nearby sweet olive and jasmine.

In lieu of an authentic antebellum mansion we suggest a Southern-inspired picnic any place where there are grass, trees or flowers. Ask the women to wear long summer dresses and picture hats to add atmosphere.

Magnolia blooms add the final touch of Southern elegance to a buffet set up on the grassy lawn at Devereaux plantation. Martha McNair serves a slice of pecan pie to one of her guests at a table laden with smoked ham, candied yams and a pair of rich desserts.

Smoked Ham

Follow this same procedure to cook chicken, turkey, duck, venison, other roasts or fowl.

1. Select a fully cooked ham, preferably boneless. Allow at least ½ pound per person, enough for tasty sandwiches later.

2. In a covered smoker or barbecue kettle with tight-fitting lid, build a mound of charcoal and ignite. When the coals are gray, distribute them around the sides. Place a pan of water in the center. This helps produce tender, juicy meat.

3. Position ham in the center of the rack. If you have a unit with double racks, cook two types of meat at once: one for now and another for the freezer or impromptu picnicking later in the week.

4. Smoke the meat for 1 hour per pound, adding charcoal whenever necessary to maintain an even low fire. Hickory or other fragrant wood chips can be added to the coals during the final cooking hour.

5. Baste the meat about once every hour with your favorite sauce or try the following tasty glaze.

Brother Mac's Glaze: Combine ½ can (6 oz.) frozen orange juice concentrate, 5 oz. bottle steak sauce, ¼ cup butter or margarine, juice from 2 lemons, 2 tablespoons each Worcestershire sauce and honey, 2 teaspoons soy sauce, 1 tablespoon brown sugar and, if desired, pressed garlic to taste. Simmer all ingredients together for at least 20 minutes. Do not allow to boil.

Makes about 1 cup glaze.

Young picnickers settle on the spacious lawns of Devereaux to enjoy an afternoon of the good food that has made Southern cooking famous. With these recipes, you can simulate the flavor of the old South even without an antebellum mansion for a backdrop.

Melon Basket

1. Draw proposed basket design on a watermelon with a pencil and cut out unwanted sections with a sharp knife.

2. Scoop out flesh with melon baller. Smooth up basket edges with knife. Prepare balls from many kinds of available melons and chill in sealed containers; chill basket.

3. Wrap basket in foil for transporting.

4. On site, combine balls in basket and add other diced fresh fruits, if desired. Garnish with lime wedges to be squeezed over melons. For a large crowd keep additional melon balls in cooler to refill basket as needed.

Serves 10.

Ruth's Angel Biscuits

Southern biscuits are legendary, but Ruth Dosher's cloudlike updated version with yeast is lighter than traditional Southern biscuits.

| 1 package active dry yeast |
| 5 tablespoons lukewarm water |
| 5 cups all-purpose flour |
| 3 tablespoons sugar |
| 5 teaspoons baking powder |
| ½ teaspoon soda |
| 1½ teaspoons salt |
| 1 cup oil |
| 2 cups buttermilk |

1. Sprinkle yeast over water and allow to soften.

2. Combine flour, sugar, baking powder, soda and salt. Add oil and mix in until it forms small pieces. Stir in buttermilk

and the softened yeast. Cover bowl and chill thoroughly. (At this point dough may be refrigerated at least 1 day before biscuits are cut out and baked.)

3. Form into ball and knead lightly on a floured board. Roll out to about ½-inch thickness. Cut with 2½-inch biscuit cutter and place barely touching in a greased cookie sheet. Allow to rise until puffy but not doubled in size in a warm place for 30 minutes to an hour or more depending upon temperature.

4. Bake in 400°F/205°C oven until lightly browned (about 10 to 15 minutes).

Makes about 4 dozen.

Note: Bake just before leaving for the picnic and wrap in foil. If this isn't possible, they're still good when cold.

Eula Cain's Pecan Pie

Eula Cain's pecan pie is sinfully delicious, lighter than many of the sticky versions.

| 3 eggs, beaten |
| ⅔ cup sugar |
| ⅓ cup melted butter or margarine |
| 1 tablespoon flour |
| 1 teaspoon vanilla |
| ¼ teaspoon salt |
| 1 cup light corn syrup |
| 1 cup pecans, halved or chopped |
| 9-inch unbaked pastry shell (your favorite recipe or frozen) |
| Whipping cream (optional) |

1. Combine all ingredients except pecans and beat until well blended. Stir in chopped pecans and pour into pie crust. Or pour filling into crust and arrange pecan halves in a circular pattern on top.

2. Bake at 375°F/190°C for about 50 minutes or until knife inserted in the center comes out clean. If the pecans start to get too brown, cover loosely with foil near end of baking. Serve warm or chilled with mounds of whipped cream.

Serves 6.

Note: Pecan pie freezes well. Prepare several to keep on hand for quick get-away picnics. You can also substitute more plentiful, less costly walnuts.

Lucille McNair's Pineapple-Strawberry Torte

A dramatic confection fit for Jefferson Davis himself, this is a big dessert and should be polished off the day it is assembled.

| 12 egg whites (at room temperature) |
| 3 cups granulated sugar |
| 1½ teaspoons white vinegar |
| ½ teaspoon salt |
| 1 teaspoon vanilla |
| 3 cups whipping cream |
| 2 tall cans (16 oz. each) crushed pineapple, well drained |
| 4 cups strawberries, thinly sliced and sweetened with sugar to taste |
| Whole strawberries and mint sprigs for garnish |

1. Beat egg whites until soft peaks form, gradually adding sugar, about ½ cup at a time. When whites form stiff peaks, add vanilla, salt and vinegar.

2. Line 3 nine-inch cake pans with waxed paper, pleating to fit sides of pan. Divide the egg white mixture equally and spread in pans. Bake at 275°F/135°C for about 1½ hours or until lightly browned. Remove meringue layers from paper liners and allow to cool. (If meringue crumbles a bit do not worry, just fill in broken spots with crumbs.)

3. Whip cream until stiff. Fold in pineapple and spread about one quarter of the whipped cream mixture on top of first layer; cover with half the sliced strawberries. Top with the second layer, another quarter of the pineapple cream and the rest of the berries. Add third layer. Ice the top and sides with remaining pineapple cream and garnish with whole strawberries and mint. Refrigerate at least 4 hours before serving or traveling to the picnic.

Serves 16 to 18.

Note: It's difficult to transport the completed torte and someone should be designated to hold it steady in a large box en route. Meringue layers can be made one or two days ahead and it may be easier to carry them wrapped in foil with the cream mixture and strawberries in plastic containers in cooler. Put it all together at the picnic site and chill in the cooler.

Alternative Menu Suggestions

● If you don't have a covered smoker, serve glazed baked ham or stop at the delicatessen for sliced Virginia ham.

● When melons are unavailable substitute a mixed fruit salad.

● If time is short, cook refrigerated canned biscuits or pick up a bakery version.

● Substitute frozen commercial pecan pie if necessary.

● A simple strawberry shortcake can pinch-hit for the more time-consuming torte. Or offer a big bowl of fresh strawberries if your guests are calorie conscious.

(See page 106 for suggestions for carrying individual dishes to the site.)

Long Sundae

Something like the Mad Hatter's tea party, this stand-up, summertime ice cream social is no humdrum affair. Easy to prepare, a snap to clean up, the Long Sundae starts with gallons of ice cream and a roll of aluminum foil and ends with a dozen or so stuffed guests, any age, plus a lot of fun and silliness.

The actual length of the sundae is determined by the number of guests, who step right up to the tables, stake out a section of ice cream and build their own sundaes on the foil in front of them. If the guest list grows, let the sundae grow. Link narrow tables end-to-end or place planks at waist height. Don't worry about chairs; everyone stands up to eat, sampling and concocting. Keep the set-up in the shade and close to the kitchen — a super sundae is no match for the summer sun.

Long Sundae for 15

Long Sundae

Toppings: Marshmallow Sauce, Strawberry Jam, Chocolate Syrup, Fudge Sauce, Butterscotch Sauce

Sliced Fruit / Chopped Nuts

Oatmeal Cookies

Lemonade

(Recipe follows)

Preparing the Table

You'll need a disposable plastic drop cloth or butcher paper and a roll or two of 20-inch wide heavy duty aluminum foil; paper napkins, plastic spoons and cups. (The foil is multipurpose — it serves as a long plate for the ice cream and helps with easy cleanup. When the picnic is over, simply toss all the used napkins, plastic cups and spoons into the middle of the foil, roll it up and throw it away.)

Ready the tables by covering them entirely with the plastic drop cloth or butcher paper. Then run overlapping strips of foil the length of the tables. Fold up the edges of the foil to form inch-high sidewalls and crimp the corners to avoid leakage.

Opposite: For an 8-yard long ice cream spectacular, we constructed a skinny tabletop of plywood on waist-high pedestals. We anticipated a last minute scramble to get the ice cream arranged before it melted. As it turned out, it was frozen so hard we had ample time. Windsocks of ripstop nylon flew from the rafters and bamboo poles.

Long Sundae

Our sundae spectacular was calculated to gorge 15 guests; adjust the amount of food according to the number you invite.

3-4 half-gallon cartons ice cream, various flavors
2 jars (7 oz. each) marshmallow topping
1 to 2 tablespoons cream or milk
1 jar (12 oz.) strawberry jam
1 large can (10 oz.) chocolate syrup
1 large can (10 oz.) fudge sauce
1 large can (10 oz.) butterscotch sauce
15 maraschino cherries with stems, drained
2 cups chopped nuts
Sliced peaches, strawberries, sherry-soaked raisins, applesauce (optional)
8 to 10 bananas

1. **The day before:** Remove carton from ice cream and cut each ½ gallon brick into 6 to 8 slices. (Use an electric carving knife or a sharp knife dipped frequently in water.) Place pieces of waxed paper between each slice to keep them separated. Repack in cartons or wrap securely and freeze solidly until serving time.

2. **Day of the picnic:** Thin marshmallow topping with small amount of cream or milk; thin strawberry jam with a little hot water. Pour syrups and sauces into pitchers; place chopped nuts in bowls.

3. If serving peaches, strawberries or other fruit, heap in bowls and cover with plastic.

4. Just before serving time, slice the bananas lengthwise into halves and reserve. Place the bowls of other fruit and toppings, pitchers of syrup and lemonade and plates of cookies in handy spots on the table.

Now is the time to be fast on your feet: with a helper close at your heels, place the ice cream slices lengthwise down the center of the foil. Working quickly, arrange lengthwise sections of bananas on the ice cream and follow with the maraschino cherries.

Now call in the crowd and reach for your camera. Every super sundae deserves a picture.
Serves 15.

Above: These ice cream connoisseurs concocted fantastic creations from the dozen flavors and the variety of toppings. Of course, everyone wanted to taste everyone else's, which led to lots of noisy activity.

Pumpkin Patch Picnic

A crisp October day offers the perfect excuse for carrying a feast to a nearby pumpkin patch. Throughout America are smaller versions of the great pumpkin harvest festivals that originated in Half Moon Bay, California, and Circleville, Ohio. Often you can harvest your own right from the growers' fields. There's no thumping involved to determine ripeness; once it's orange, a pumpkin is ready to use. Take home several for Halloween carving, Thanksgiving pies and repeats of our Hot Pumpkin Soup.

With the farmer's permission you can nestle a picnic among pumpkins still on the vine or, as we did, stage your meal in the midst of the golden harvest.

Pumpkin Patch Picnic for 6

Hot Pumpkin Soup

Chicken-Mushroom Turnovers

Olives
Apple Spice Cake

Mulled Cider

(Recipe follows)

As the October sun sets over a field of golden pumpkins, these picnickers prepare to carry home their empty picnic hamper plus a few pumpkins purchased from the farmer for holiday carving and cooking. If children are along on your picnic, the afternoon can be spent carving jack-o-lanterns to carry home. Children too young to handle a knife love to attach long carrots for noses, radish eyes, string bean lips and parsley hair. Stick vegetables on pumpkins with toothpicks.

Hot Pumpkin Soup

For dramatic effect, serve from a baked pumpkin shell (directions follow).

1 medium onion, chopped

½ cup chopped green onions

3 tablespoons butter

½ teaspoon each **ground ginger and nutmeg**

3 cups canned pumpkin

5 cups chicken stock or broth

2 cups whipping cream

Salt and freshly ground pepper to taste.

Baked pumpkin shell (optional)

Croutons or sour cream

1. Sauté onions in butter until transparent. Add spices. Combine onion mixture and canned pumpkin in a blender or food processor until smooth.

2. Return pumpkin mixture to a large saucepan and stir in broth. Bring to a boil before adding cream, salt and pepper. Simmer for about 15 minutes, but do not allow to boil.

Serves 6.

Note: Transport hot soup in a preheated thermos. If you prepare it the day before, reheat slowly, but do not allow to boil. At picnic, pour soup into baked pumpkin shell. Garnish bowls or mugs of soup with herb-flavored croutons or dollops of sour cream, and small scoops of baked pumpkin from inside the shell.

Baked Pumpkin Shell:
Wash a pumpkin no smaller than 10 inches in diameter. Cut off top for a lid. Scoop out and discard the seeds, strings and pulp, leaving a wall at least 1 inch thick. Replace lid, wrapping stem in foil to prevent burning, and place in a shallow pan with about ½-inch water. Bake at 350°F/180°C until barely tender, and still firm, about 1 hour. Wrap entire pumpkin in several layers of foil.

Serves 6.

Chicken-Mushroom Turnovers

Turnovers are easy to make if you start with frozen puff pastry dough. Substitute any leftover meat for the chicken filling and combine with favorite herbs and spices, cheese, cooked vegetables or compatible leftovers.

Filling: Sauté ½ pound chopped fresh mushrooms and ¼ cup minced onion in 3 tablespoons butter or margarine. Combine with 2 cups cooked chicken, finely chopped, 3 tablespoons minced parsley, ¼ teaspoon dried tarragon, salt and freshly ground pepper to taste.

Pastry: Thaw two 10-ounce packages frozen patty shells (6 per package). On a floured board roll out each patty shell to about an 8-inch circle or to ⅛-inch thickness. Add about ¼ cup filling in center of circle. Fold over, moisten edges of pastry with water and press together with a fork to seal. Position on ungreased baking sheets and pierce top of each turnover with a fork. Bake at 400°F/205°C until golden, about 20 minutes.

Makes 12.

Note: For hot turnovers, bake just before leaving home and wrap tightly in foil. But they're equally good cold and can be made several days ahead and frozen.

Apple Spice Cake

This plain, spicy favorite is easy to carry in its own pan. Dress it up with caramel icing, if you wish.

1 cup chopped pecans

3 cups chopped raw apples

1½ cups salad oil

2 cups sugar

2 eggs

1 teaspoon each **salt and baking soda**

2 teaspoons baking powder

2 teaspoons cinnamon

1 teaspoon each **ground cloves and allspice**

½ teaspoon ginger

2½ cups flour

1 teaspoon vanilla

1. Chop pecans and apples, set aside.

2. Measure oil into bowl; add sugar and eggs. Mix well until creamy.

3. Sift dry ingredients together and gradually add to oil mixture, blending well after each addition. Mix in vanilla. Fold chopped pecans and apples into batter. Spread evenly in greased 10-inch tube or bundt pan. Bake at 350°F/180°C for 55 to 60 minutes, until cake tests done when a bamboo skewer is inserted in the thickest part. Remove pan to cooling rack. When cool, spread top with your favorite caramel icing, if desired.

Makes 10 to 12 servings.

In the middle of the pumpkin harvest, autumn's brilliant colors are echoed in the food and accessories arranged on a hay bale. The cole slaw of purple cabbage, orange carrots and red peppers glows like neon in the bright October sun. Chicken turnovers can be made ahead and served cold along with hot pumpkin soup transfered from a thermos into a pre-baked pumpkin shell.

Mulled Cider

At home, prepare enough of this bone-warming drink to last the whole day.

1. Simply pour 3 quarts apple cider into large saucepan, add a sliced orange, a sliced lemon, a stick of cinnamon and a few cloves.

2. Heat for about 15 minutes, but do not boil.

Serves 6.

Mardi Gras Feast

First-time visitors to New Orleans usually come away delighted with the discovery of the grand cuisine of southern Louisiana. Creole cookery is deeply rooted in the French cooking of the area's first colonists. It is unique, also, because of the marriage of the natural ingredients of land and sea, and the magical spices and cooking methods of the Spanish and Africans who found homes in the bayou country.

You don't need to travel to New Orleans at Mardi Gras to enjoy a picnic with Creole flavor. This gumbo-based meal can be enjoyed anywhere, anytime, with or without the carnival trimmings. Stage a picnic, indoors or out, on Mardi Gras day or Fat Tuesday, the day before Ash Wednesday and the beginning of Lent. Invite guests to come in colorful carnival costumes, put out a huge pot of spicy Creole gumbo and join the celebration of this noisy, joyous festival.

Mardi Gras Feast for 12
Chicken and Seafood Okra Gumbo

Steamed Rice
Marinated Green Beans
French Bread
New Orleans King Cake

Beer / Café au Lait

(Recipe follows)

Spicy, colorful creole gumbo competed with costumed revelers for the spotlight at our midday picnic planned for a French Quarter balcony overlooking the colorful congestion of the Mardi Gras in New Orleans. Adapt the spirit of carnival to your own Fat Tuesday feastday, anywhere. The gumbo can be made ahead for a picnic that's easy on the partygiver.

Chicken and Seafood Okra Gumbo

Gumbo is a hearty soup thickened with either okra or filé, powdered sassafras root known to the Choctaw Indians of Louisiana as "kombo". Okra is added early in the soup preparation; if filé is used it is put in at the last minute, after the pot is taken off the heat. If you decide not to use okra in the following recipe, you may add filé powder just before serving. Once filé has been added, never allow gumbo to boil.

There are almost as many versions of gumbo as there are cooks in southern Louisiana. It can be made from any fowl, sausage, bacon, ham, seafood, game or whatever meat is available. After many years of New Orleans eating, this recipe is the author's favorite.

| 1 cup salad oil |
| 1 cup flour |
| 8 stalks celery, chopped |
| 3 large onions, chopped |
| 1 green pepper, chopped |
| ½ cup chopped parsley |
| 2 cloves garlic, minced |
| 1 pound okra, sliced |
| 2 tablespoons oil |
| 2 quarts chicken broth |
| 2 quarts water |
| ½ cup Worcestershire sauce |
| 6 drops Tabasco, add cautiously to taste |
| ½ cup catsup |
| 1 large ripe tomato, chopped |
| 2 tablespoons salt |
| 1 large slice ham, about 1 pound, chopped |
| 2 bay leaves |
| ½ teaspoon each thyme and rosemary |
| ¼ teaspoon red pepper flakes, or to taste |
| 2 cups cooked chicken, chopped |
| 2 pounds cooked crab meat, flaked |
| 3 pounds cooked shrimp, shelled and deveined |
| 2 jars (8 oz. each) oysters |
| 2 tablespoons brown sugar or molasses to taste |
| Juice of 1 lemon |
| 1 tablespoon filé (available at gourmet groceries), if okra is not used |

1. In the largest stockpot you can find, 1½ to 2 gallon capacity, make a roux by blending the salad oil and flour over low heat for about 30 minutes or until dark brown, stirring constantly.

2. Add celery, onions, green pepper, parsley and garlic. Cook, stirring frequently for 45 minutes to 1 hour.

3. Fry okra in the 2 tablespoons oil in frying pan until browned, then add to gumbo mixture. (At this stage, the mixture can be cooled and refrigerated up to 48 hours, or frozen for later use.)

4. Add chicken broth, water, Worcestershire, Tabasco, catsup, tomato, salt, ham, bay leaves, thyme, rosemary and red pepper. Simmer 3 or 4 hours.

5. About 30 minutes before serving time or leaving for picnic, add chicken, crab, shrimp and simmer just until heated through. Stir in oysters and their liquid during the final 10 minutes of simmering. Add sugar or molasses and lemon juice. If you have not used okra, add filé at this point. Taste and correct seasonings. Serve over mounds of boiled or steamed rice in large soup bowls.

Serves 12.

Note: Gumbo can be made the day before and reheated slowly. Do not allow it to boil. Carry to the site in large wide-mouthed thermos jugs or wrap the large stockpot in several layers of newspaper. If there is access to fire at the picnic site, reheat the pot of gumbo upon arrival.

Garish purple, green and gold colored sugar decorate a New Orleans king cake that's served with steaming café au lait. Colorful beads and doubloons are thrown from Mardi Gras parade floats and French Quarter balconies on carnival day.

New Orleans King Cake

Based on a Middle Ages custom brought to Louisiana by early French settlers, a colorfully decorated coffeecake is served on Twelfth Night (January 6), the official start of the carnival season. Inside the cake is a hidden treasure — a bean, a pecan half or a tiny baby doll. The finder is declared king or queen for a week and is required to provide a new "king cake" to be served the same group the following week. The custom is celebrated by families, friends or office groups, continuing until Mardi Gras.

In New Orleans king cakes come from the bakeries. But you can bake and decorate your own favorite yeast dough coffee cake to look like an oval-shaped, jeweled crown. The treasure can be baked inside the dough or tucked into a secret slit cut in the underside of the finished cake.

1. Mix your favorite sweet yeast coffeecake dough to serve 12. Let rise, then shape into an oval ring on a cooky sheet. Bake as directed in your cake recipe, until dough is lightly browned. Ice and decorate cake.

Serves 12.

Decoration: While the cake bakes prepare colored sugar in green, purple and gold. For each color, mix a dab of food-coloring pastes (available in bakery supply stores or by mail order, see page 93) with 4 to 5 tablespoons granulated sugar. Rub with fingers to evenly color the sugar. Set each color aside in separate container.

Icing: Combine 2½ cups confectioners sugar, 2 tablespoons lemon juice, 3 tablespoons water. Stir until smooth, adding up to 3 tablespoons more water until spreadable. Smooth icing over top of cake, letting some run down sides. Sprinkle immediately with colored sugar to form wide bands of green, purple and gold. Imbed pieces of candied pineapple, cherries and citron around the cake to simulate jewels.

Note: A king cake is easy to carry — just wrap in foil.

Café au Lait

1. In a drip coffee pot, make a strong brew of New Orleans roast with chicory or dark French roast, using 1 cup ground coffee and 9 cups water. Combine 6 cups milk and 3 cups half-and-half in a saucepan, bring just to boiling point and immediately remove from heat. Pour hot coffee and milk into separate thermal containers.

2. Traditionally, equal parts coffee and hot milk are poured simultaneously into mugs, but proportions should vary according to personal taste. Add sugar if you like.

Serves 12.

Note: To vary quantity of coffee to be served, use 2 tablespoons ground coffee for each ¾ cup water.

Sandwiching

Pan bagnat

Although other civilizations enjoyed versions of the sandwich for centuries, an Englishman, the fourth Earl of Sandwich, gets the credit for inventing the hand-held meal as we know it. However, we Americans have adopted sandwiches as our very own, creating an unparalleled culinary art form. Sandwiches in every conceivable combination probably go on more American picnics than any other food.

Possibilities for sandwiching are infinite. We have adapted varied ideas from all over the world. Everyone of us has favorite concoctions that travel well to picnics, but here are some new ideas and new ways with old favorites.

Oversize Sandwiches

For oversize sandwiches, to share with several friends, bake or buy a round or oblong loaf of bread. Place on a cardboard cut to shape, or rest on a cutting board that's transportable. Slice in two pieces horizontally, scoop out some of the bread and reserve for bread crumbs for use later.

1. Spread halves with any selected filling. Wrap well and chill.

2. At the site, cut round loaf into wedges or slice oblong loaf across.

The same idea can be used for a hot sandwich: fill the bread with a favorite meat loaf mixture, wrap in foil and bake at 350°F/180°C for 2 hours. Open foil to allow steam to escape, then rewrap. For warm sandwiches, serve within 3 hours.

Stuffed loaf

Pan Bagnat

For the classic French-inspired pan bagnat, slice a large oblong or round loaf of French bread in half horizontally. Remove some bread from each half, leaving about 1½-inch walls.

1. Sprinkle inside of both pieces with olive oil.

2. Layer bottom half with tomatoes, anchovy fillets, sliced ripe olives, thinly sliced onions, green pepper strips, sliced hard-cooked eggs and capers. Sprinkle with minced parsley and tarragon or basil.

3. Cover with top half, press together lightly and wrap. Cut into portions at the site.

Crêpe Stack

1. Crêpes are another bread substitute. Make thin crêpes, about 3 per person. (Crêpes can be made well ahead, frozen, then thawed to room temperature when needed.) Spread each with mayonnaise or a mixture of sour cream and minced herbs, lemon juice, salt.

2. Layer as you would

Italian Hero

1. The Italian hero is a variation on the pan bagnat. Use a long loaf of Italian bread, slice horizontally and drizzle inside with olive oil.

2. Stuff with layers of salami, bologna, mortadella, prosciutto, ham or other cold cuts and two or three kinds of sliced cheeses. Top with roasted sweet peppers, a few anchovies and hot pepper pods, if desired. Drizzle lightly with vinegar, add salt and pepper to taste. Wrap tightly. Cut into sections at the picnic.

Lettuce sandwich

a cake, alternating with 2 or 3 compatible fillings such as crab salad or chopped olives with cream cheese, or fill the stack with cold cuts and

Pourboire Variation

The pourboire, or "po boy" to New Orleanians, is a variation on both the pan bagnat and hero, using a long, skinny individual French loaf. Spread horizontally cut halves with mayonnaise and fill with any desired filling, from fried oysters to ham and cheese.

Dieters' Sandwiches

Treat dieters to breadless sandwiches. Spread filling on large leaves of rinsed and chilled romaine lettuce, or wrap any kind of smaller lettuce leaves around a selected filling.

cheese. Top with an unfilled crêpe; wrap tightly and chill up to 24 hours. At the picnic cut into wedges as you would a pie.

Crêpe stack

Pocket Sandwiches

1. Pita or Arab pocket bread (see page 55), large or small, in halves or whole with a small opening cut, are perfect for stuffing with almost any fare — cold cuts, cheeses, meat and fish salads, avocado and to-mato, Mediterranean fried falafels, warm, cooked stewed meats, vegetables, and on and on and on.

Pita pocket

Fancy Shapes and Loaves

"Fancy sandwiches" always implies trimmed-away crusts — often the best part of the bread. There are occasions, however, when fancy sandwiches seem just right.

1. Trim away crusts from an unsliced white or wheat loaf. Slice horizontally into four layers, spreading each with butter.

2. Layer like a cake with one filling, or a compatible combination such as chicken salad, egg salad and spicy ham salad. Top with the final bread layer, buttered side down.

3. Frost entire loaf with fluffy cream cheese beaten until very light with a bit of milk. Chill. When ready to serve, cut thinly with a serrated knife into 14 to 18 slices depending on size of loaf.

Fancy variations: For colorful pinwheels, slice an uncut loaf lengthwise as thinly as possible, trim away crusts. Butter and spread to the edges with filling, then roll up as you would a jellyroll. Fasten with wooden picks or small bamboo skewers and wrap tightly in plastic wrap. Just before serving time, remove picks and cut crosswise into thin slices.

For finger rolls, use sliced white bread, trim crusts, spread slices with filling and roll each separately. Wrap very tightly with foil or plastic wrap and chill overnight. Garnish each end with a sprig of watercress or parsley before serving.

Pinwheel

Bagel and lox

Brioche and pâté

International Samples

Some of the world's best sandwiches are also the simplest. Open-faced smørrebrød of Denmark are unsurpassed. Spread rye, pumpernickel or other good fresh bread with lots of softened butter. Top with bits of herring, smoked eel, halved tiny meatballs, sardines, cold veal, smoked salmon or pâté. Garnish tops with a twist of lemon or cucumber, berries, chopped chives, herb sprigs, radish slices, or a bit of pickle.

■ Broodjes from Holland are small, soft white rolls, slathered with sweet butter and filled with any preferred sandwich makings. It's the butter and very fresh rolls that make broodjes great.

■ Imitate the French method of filling a horizontally split baguette of fresh crusty bread with plenty of creamy butter, thin slices of superb ham — and nothing else. Or try a rich, buttery brioche roll or croissant simply smothered in the finest pâté.

■ Simple English tea sandwiches described on page 45 are another pleasure of the sandwich world.

■ Don't forget an old delicatessen classic — chewy water bagels, split and smeared generously with cream cheese, topped with smoked salmon and onion.

Tips for Sandwich Making

☐ The cardinal rule for good sandwiches is that they are only as good as the components. Always use the best bread available, homebaked if possible, and the freshest and purest ingredients.

☐ Leave crust on bread to prevent drying (unless you are making a fancy loaf or rolled sandwiches). Spread room-temperature butter, cream cheese, peanut butter or other soft spread all the way to the edges of each slice.

☐ The fresh taste of home-made mayonnaise for spreading or mixing cannot be duplicated by commercial products. And it's so easy to prepare. See the recipe on page 65 for a blender version. After the addition of the oil, add any of the following and blend a few seconds longer: chopped capers, green onions, lemon juice, mustard, curry powder, cayenne or any favorite herb or spice.

☐ As a change of pace from the usual lettuce, add spinach leaves, alfalfa sprouts, sprigs of watercress, thinly sliced cucumbers, shredded cabbage or cole slaw.

☐ If your sandwiches call for moist salad fillings or mayonnaise, spread inside surfaces of both slices of bread with butter to help prevent sogginess. Or transport ingredients separately and construct them on the site.

☐ Sandwiches transport best in plastic boxes or containers with tight-fitting lids. In lieu of these, wrap securely with foil, waxed paper or plastic wrap. If you make several kinds of sandwiches, label them as you wrap to avoid confusion at the picnic.

Caution: Except on very cold days, fillings with mayonnaise, eggs and cream cheese should be kept in an ice cooler until ready to serve.

A Few Sandwich Fillings

☐ Avocado with shrimp and green onions (sprinkle avocado with lemon or lime juice to prevent darkening)

☐ Avocado, tomatoes, alfalfa sprouts

☐ Cream cheese or cottage cheese with crushed pineapple, banana and mango

☐ Cream cheese with chopped walnuts or pecans

☐ Cream cheese with minced ripe olives

☐ Cream cheese with shrimp, minced onion and cayenne

☐ Deviled egg with chopped ham, watercress or cucumber slices

☐ Hearts of palm with herbed mayonnaise

☐ Herbed cheese spread with crumbled bacon

☐ Pâté with thinly sliced onion and tomatoes

☐ Peanut butter with raisins and bacon

☐ Peanut butter with chopped dates and honey

☐ Pork roast slices with applesauce and thinly sliced onions

☐ Roquefort cheese with green onions

☐ Smoked salmon with green pepper, onions, lemon juice, pickles and mayonnaise

☐ Sliced roast chicken with bacon, spinach and sliced mushrooms

☐ Sliced roast duck with orange marmalade

☐ Sardines puréed with mayonnaise and olives

☐ Steak tartare with anchovies or caviar

☐ Tuna mixed with mashed avocado, green onions, peppers, mayonnaise and horseradish

☐ Tuna mixed with cream cheese and lemon juice, sliced olives and chopped almonds

☐ Tuna mixed with chopped chutney, raisins, apple, macadamia nuts, olives

☐ Tomatoes with Italian pesto sauce

☐ Turkey slices with cranberry sauce and watercress

☐ Veal roast slices with anchovies and chives

Supersandwich for a Crowd

For a super extravagant variation on the sandwich theme, construct a 6-foot version that feeds 20 people, or build one to any length you need. Your only limitation is the size of the station wagon (or station wagon **and** trailer!) slated to transport your supersandwich.

Supersandwich for a Crowd
Supersandwich

Tomato Soup
Raw Vegetables
Potato Chips
Oatmeal Cookies
Soft Drinks, Beer, Coffee

(Recipe follows)

Right: Yvan and Stephanie were given the awesome responsibility of transporting our 9-foot long supersandwich from the van to the picnic site. To create the length we cut the heels from nine large loaves of French bread and buttered them together to form one continuous loaf on a board. Then the bread was split horizontally and filled. We removed the protective foil wrapping just for the camera. Tied inside Jay's red and white *furoshiki* (see page 99) are chips, paper plates, napkins and other supplies

Left: Superphotographer Tom Tracy takes a superbite from a section of the supersandwich. It turned out that our big sandwich fed about 35 people.

Many bakeries will prepare 6-foot loaves of French, rye, pumpernickel or other breads if you order several days in advance. If special order loaves are too short at 6 feet, too costly, or unavailable, there is an alternative. It's possible to create the same heroic proportions by using several long loaves of unsliced bread, cutting away the rounded ends and placing them together to form a loaf as long as you wish.

Have ready a 1 by 10-inch board (cut several inches longer than your planned sandwich) on which to assemble and transport the loaf. Leave board plain, paint it, or wrap in foil or colorful vinyl.

1. Begin supersandwich construction by arranging loaves end-to-end on the board. Slice lengthwise, leaving the bottom halves a bit thicker than the tops. Using your fingers, scoop some bread from the bottom pieces to form depressions to hold the fillings. (And cut down on the quantity of bread consumed.)

2. The sandwich can be stuffed with one kind

of filling, or several that change about every two feet as you go along. Prepare your favorite fillings in quantity and assemble as you would an ordinary sandwich. You might wish to turn out a superhero by stacking on various cold meats, cheeses, onions, lettuce, tomatoes and peppers sprinkled with Italian salad dressing.

3. After completing the masterpiece, decorate the board with clusters of fresh vegetables. Plant flags on skewers to indicate where to cut for various sandwich fillings.

Most picnickers will want to sample a section of each.

4. For transporting the giant, cover the finished loaf or loaves with plastic wrap and tuck under the bottom to keep the fillings from escaping. Finally, wrap the entire sandwich in foil. If the weather is on the cool side, accompany with hot soup or a warm drink. Hot weather calls for a chilled soup and icy beverages.

Note: Almost as important to pack as the supersandwich itself are the sharp knives for cutting it.

A cross section of the supersandwich shows layers of varied cold cuts and cheeses on buttered bread. At the site we offered lettuce leaves, sliced tomatoes, avocado slices, alfalfa sprouts, olives, mayonnaise, mustard and relish for guests to add as they pleased.

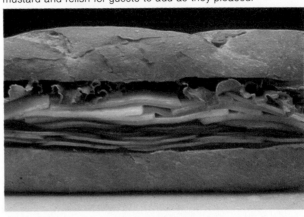

Around-the-World Outdoor Meals

The attraction of fresh air combined with good food and good company is universal. The French sip their wines and spread creamy Camembert cheese onto fresh crusty baguettes. Middle Easterners savor lemony lamb and rice wrapped in grape leaves. Germans picnic on their wursts, pumpernickel and dark beer; the Italians enjoy their **frittata** al fresco; the Chinese their pot stickers. From the lakes high in the Swiss Alps to the beaches of Australia, the picnic hamper has universal appeal.

Opposite: This Japanese garden on a glorious spring day could be in Kyoto, but it's really in San Francisco. One of the pleasures of picnicking is to borrow an available nearby landscape and recreate the mood and taste of another part of the world. Mark and Vickie chose a serene spot in a tea garden and for an hour or so enjoyed the cherry blossoms at their peak. Above: The lacquered box is filled with *sushi* and other Japanese delicacies selected from a restaurant.

When you travel abroad, visit local food marketplaces and gather the specialties from several sellers. What better way to really learn about a country's cuisine? Then find a public square, park or scenic attraction and spread a picnic. Most of us remember these impromptu outings among the best meals of our travels, and considerably less expensive than similar dishes served in restaurants.

World travelers can luck upon public picnics such as the famed Oktoberfest in Germany set up under canvas canopies, the long tables loaded with beer, sausages, smoked chicken, potato salad and sauerkraut. There's music and dancing into the night.

At home you can create your very own Oktoberfest under the canopy of autumn leaves. Add an accordionist, German costumes and pretend you're reveling in Munich for an afternoon.

Throw a fiesta and you can be transported to carnival in Rio. Or create an instant Japan by packing a picnic of **sushi** rice from a Japanese restaurant and heading for a place where fruit trees are in bloom.

In this chapter you'll find picnic plans with menus, international recipes and ideas for serving. There are suggestions, too, for activities and nearby scenic places where you can go to recreate some of the world's best picnic experiences. These ideas are to help you capture the mood of international picnicking. Once you get the idea of how it's done, refer to international cookbooks for ethnic cuisines and invent your own outdoor events. Many of the food items are available in specialty food stores, often by mail order.

Don't feel you have to stage an elaborate scene to enjoy these international foods. They taste almost as good right out of a picnic hamper on a strip of grassy lawn as they do in a showy setup. But this collection of picnics proves worth the effort that goes into them. They're great alternatives to typical tuna sandwiches or fried chicken to go.

French Fare Lunch

Many of the fine foods of France lend themselves to a lunch on the green — a **déjeuner sur l'herbe.** All that's really required for a grand French picnic is a crusty loaf of bread, some good cheese and a bottle of wine. We've added a cold melange of vegetables from Provence, **ratatouille,** that can be made a day or two ahead, pâté from the delicatessen or made from a recipe in your French cookbook, fresh asparagus cooked tender-crisp and served in a vinaigrette sauce, and, of course, a plate of rich French pastries from a bakery.

French Lunch for 4

Ratatouille

Pâté / Baguette of French Bread

Asparagus Vinaigrette

French Cheeses: Brie, Boursin,
Camembert, Roquefort

Assorted French Pastries

Red Wine

(Recipe follows)

Ratatouille
(Vegetable Stew)

The flavor of this vegetable stew is better if made a day or two ahead.

It can be slowly reheated very successfully, but is actually most delicious served cold. Make enough ratatouille for a stay-at-home treat with leftovers to fold inside hot crêpes for a picnic later in the week. If you wish to turn the dish into a hearty meal, add sliced grilled sausages during the final stage of cooking or reheating.

2 to 3 tablespoons olive oil
1 large onion, thinly sliced
1 green or red pepper, seeded and sliced
2 cloves garlic, mashed
2 ripe tomatoes, peeled, seeded and chopped
½ teaspoon each **salt and dried basil**
¼ teaspoon each **dried rosemary and thyme**
½ cup olive oil
1 large eggplant (about 1½ lbs.) peeled and diced
2 medium zucchini, sliced
Freshly ground pepper and salt to taste

1. Heat the oil in a large heavy saucepan or Dutch oven and sauté onions and pepper until soft, but not browned, about 10 minutes. Stir in garlic, tomatoes and herbs. Cook uncovered, very slowly, over low heat for about 10 minutes more, or until juice from tomato is almost gone.

2. In a skillet, heat scant ½ cup oil and sauté eggplant about 1 cup at a time until lightly browned; add more olive oil as needed. Remove and add to the onion-tomato mixture. Sauté zucchini in the same manner, adding to the mixture as ready.

3. Add pepper and more salt if needed, cover and simmer over low heat for about 10 minutes. Uncover, raise heat very slightly and continue cooking for about 20 minutes more, or until juices have evaporated. Tip pot several times and baste vegetables with their juices. Watch carefully to see that heat is not too high. Do not scorch vegetables in bottom of pot. (Recipe may be doubled successfully.)

Serves 4.

Note: Ratatouille can go to the picnic in an earthenware pot and a casserole carrier (see page 106).

A wire shopping basket from France is a sturdy, handsome picnic carrier. Line the bottom with a tablecloth or dishtowel to prevent small items from escaping. For *déjeuner sur l'herbe* there is asparagus in vinaigrette dressing and cold ratatouille, both in plastic containers with tight-fitting lids, several imported cheeses, a wedge of truffled pâté from the delicatessen, a baguette of crusty sweet French bread, chilled white imported wine and mouth-watering pastries from a bakery. Carry along a few flowers cut from your garden for atmosphere.

English Tea on the Green

English picnicking became fashionable during the early nineteenth century as the result of the formation of the Picnic Society of London. To this day the English are probably the most passionate picnickers on the planet. They possess a special knack for packing a basket and dining with great elegance in the picturesque countryside.

Society stops at the great London food halls of Harrods or Fortnum & Mason for ready-to-go cold picnic staples — champagne, smoked salmon, Cornish pasties, potted shrimps, game pies, Scotch eggs, pheasant, water biscuits and Cheshire cheese. Then it's off to the races or just a drive through the country, the hamper filled with delectable morsels, good china and heirloom silverware.

All of the English seem to seize every chance for a picnic. Holidays and Sundays find the greens and public gardens of London and small villages alike dotted with hampers. Along with good food, there's always soccer, handball, cricket, bird watching, nature walks, flower shows, or concerts.

We chose to combine two great English customs — the picnic and the afternoon tea, usually taken indoors. Tea in England is certainly more than just a hot drink: it's a late afternoon meal. High tea to the city dweller can mean a stylishly served spread of little sandwiches, cakes, fancy pastries and biscuits of all types. Rural English often refer to high tea as "meat tea," and add cooked fish and meat dishes to the menu for a heartier meal.

Of course, you don't need a Bentley and expensive table service to enjoy a day in the country, English-style. Pack a hamper with inexpensive ware, good things to eat, and load it into the Ford or Fiat, Dodge or Datsun. Whether you go simply or elaborately, don't overlook the pleasures of a proper teatime in the most restful spot you can find.

English Tea for 4

Tea Sandwiches

Scottish Scones / Jams and Jellies

Strawberries with Devon Cream

English Crackers / Sliced Cheeses

Scottish Shortbread

Dundee Cake

Assorted Pastries

Hot Tea:

Earl Grey, English Breakfast, or Darjeeling

(Recipe follows)

Out comes the English-made, fitted picnic hamper from a vintage Bentley touring car parked on a little orchard lane. The springtime setting is California, but it certainly has some of the feeling of the English countryside in April. Packed inside the hamper are all the necessities and more for afternoon tea: china and silver from Tiffany, little tea sandwiches, homebaked dundee cake and Scottish shortbread, scones (see page 47) and marmalades, strawberries and cream, cookies from Fortnum & Mason. And behind the scenes, there's a small portable stove to heat water for a proper pot of tea.

Tea Sandwiches

1. Select thinly sliced bread, trim away crusts, then cut into small triangles, finger shapes, squares or rounds.

2. Spread with softened butter, then add any filling. Cover with top slice of bread or leave open-face and garnish with olive slices, tiny shrimp, bits of green onion, watercress leaves or other attractive bits of color.

Suggested fillings:
☐ Thinly sliced, peeled cucumbers, (crisped in ice water, then drained and dried with paper towels)

☐ Softened cream cheese blended with marmalade, deviled ham, chopped nuts or chopped olives

☐ Deviled egg salad with crumbled bacon, grated cheese or minced olives

☐ Sliced ham with chutney

☐ Sliced breast of chicken with watercress

☐ Any meat or fish salad mixture

Scottish Scones

Early Scots baked scones on a flat griddle over the embers of an open fire.

2 cups flour
2½ teaspoons baking powder
3 tablespoons sugar
½ teaspoon salt
¼ cup butter
2 eggs, beaten
½ cup buttermilk
Sugar (optional)

1. Sift flour with baking powder, sugar and salt. Cut in butter until size of small peas. Add eggs and buttermilk, combining mixture until just moistened.

2. Turn onto lightly floured board, knead gently, handling as little as possible. Pat or roll out ½ inch thick. With floured knife, cut into diamond shapes, or cut rounds with cookie cutter.

3. Place on greased baking sheet, about 1 inch apart. Sprinkle with additional sugar, if you wish. Bake in 425°F/220°C oven for 15 to 20 minutes or until golden.

Makes about 12.

Opposite: Tea table linens are spread on the new spring grass amongst the wildflowers. (First put down a plastic drop cloth to protect against grass stains and dampness.) Cushions provide picnickers Lenny, Christine and Craig with comfortable seating. The strawberries, cream, milk for tea and the little sandwiches were carried in a small ice chest. Pastries on top of the hamper are from a special bakery and the plaid tin box hold our version of Scottish shortbread.

Strawberries with Devon Cream

Along with its violets and green countryside, Devon is noted for its heavy clotted cream, a delicate regional specialty that is hard to reproduce outside Devonshire. However, you can simulate a tasty imitation with readily available ingredients.

1. Soften 8 ounces cream cheese, then beat with ¼ cup sugar and ⅓ cup sour cream until smooth. Chill.

2. To serve, mound cream in center of plate and surround with fresh washed strawberries. Devon cream is also tasty spread on scones, muffins, or other tea cakes.

Makes about 1⅓ cups.

Scottish Shortbread

Butter-rich shortbread keeps well if stored in airtight tins.

½ cup sugar
2 cups all-purpose flour
½ cup cornstarch
½ teaspoon salt
1 cup (½ lb.) butter, chilled
Sugar

1. Sift sugar, flour, cornstarch and salt together. Cut butter into small pieces and blend into the sugar mixture with a pastry blender or two knives. Do not use hands, butter should stay as cold as possible. Form into a ball and refrigerate for 30 minutes.

2. Flatten chilled dough to ½-inch thickness, patting into shallow, greased and floured 8 by 8-inch baking pans or 8-inch cake pans.

3. With a fork, pierce to define shapes for the finished shortbread — triangles, strips, squares or wedges. Make further indentation in the dough along the dotted line with a knife. Place in preheated 450°F/230°C oven for 5 minutes; reduce heat to 350°F/180°C and bake up to 30 minutes more. Check every 10 minutes and remove when the shortbread starts to turn pale gold. Remove from oven and sprinkle with sugar. Cool and cut on indicated lines before removing from pans.

Makes about 1½ dozen cookies.

Hot Tea

1. Tea is best made at the picnic site, otherwise it gets too strong en route. At home bring to a full boil plenty of fresh cold water and pour into preheated thermoses. If there's a heat source at the picnic area, boil water after you arrive.

2. Pour a bit of hot water into a china or glass teapot and rinse it out to take off the chill. Place 1 teaspoon of loose tea in the pot for every cup of water you plan to add, plus an extra teaspoon for the pot. Add boiling water and steep about 3 minutes, more or less, according to taste.

3. Open the lid and give the leaves one stir, then pour through a strainer into cups. Provide a container of hot water so that each person can correct the strength to taste. The English usually add milk (lemon-tea is often considered American). Some insist that the milk be poured into the cup before the tea, others add it last. Sweeten with sugar, if desired.

Dundee Cake

Scotland once again gets the credit for this tea classic.

1 cup butter, softened
1 cup sugar
5 eggs
2½ cups all-purpose flour
¼ teaspoon each **salt and baking soda**
⅔ cup each **currants and raisins**
¾ cup chopped mixed candied fruit
1½ tablespoons grated lemon rind
½ cup chopped almonds
¾ cup whole blanched almonds
⅓ cup candied cherries, halved

1. Cream butter and sugar, then add eggs, one at a time, beating well after each addition.

2. Combine flour, salt, soda, currants, raisins, candied fruit, lemon rind and chopped almonds. Stir into batter.

3. Spread mixture evenly in greased and floured 9-inch springform pan. Decorate with whole almonds and cherries. Bake at 300°F/150°C for 1½ hours or until skewer inserted in center comes out clean. Cool 5 minutes in pan, then unmold and cool on rack.

Serves 12 to 16.

Note: Dundee cake freezes well. Divide into wedges, wrap and freeze for several teas to come.

Almond-studded and buttery, Dundee cake is a favorite, even of those who usually do not care for fruit cake. For small teatime picnics divide a large cake into wedges and freeze individually. It thaws enroute.

Spanish Sherry Picnic

The Spanish, with their sunny climate, are great picnickers, matching vigorous appetites to hearty foods. Chef Jose Pons, now a Californian, offers a menu and original recipes based on his childhood memories of picnicking in Spain.

Picnic From Spain for 3 or more

Tortilla de Patata

Ensalade de Tomate

Pollo Frito

Emparadado de Jamon

Empanada Gallega

Brazo de Gítano

Sherry / Coffee

(Recipes follow)

Chef Jose Pons prepares a *Tortilla de Patata* in the kitchen of his El Greco restaurant in San Anselmo, California. He created the recipes for our picnic based on traditional menus for outdoor eating in Spain.

Tortilla de Patata
(Potato Omelet)

Unlike the Mexican tortilla, this Tortilla de Patata is a simple omelet of potatoes and onions. It is one of Spain's most popular dishes, enjoyed hot or cold. Olive oil used instead of butter provides authentic flavor. Slices of cold tortilla are often eaten between slices of bread, an idea to adapt for a simple picnic accompanied with fruit and wine.

½ cup olive oil
3 medium-size potatoes, peeled and sliced thin
Salt
1 medium onion, chopped
4 eggs
2 tablespoons olive oil

1. Heat ½ cup oil in heavy 10-inch frying pan over moderate heat. Add potatoes; salt well and turn to cover with oil.

2. Cook 10 minutes, add onion and continue cooking until potatoes are slightly browned. Remove from frying pan and place in colander over bowl to drain excess oil. Reserve the oil.

3. In large mixing bowl, beat eggs slightly; add drained potatoes and onions. In frying pan place reserved oil plus enough more to measure 2 tablespoons. Heat oil; add egg mixture and cook about 2 minutes.

4. When omelet is firm but not dry, turn it over by placing a plate on top of the pan, then inverting it to turn the omelet onto the plate. Slide omelet back into frying pan and cook another 3 minutes to brown the underside.

Serves 4.

Empanada Gallega
(Pork and Chicken Pie)

Take this hearty pizza-like pie to a picnic or serve it at home as a simple main dish.

Yeast Dough (recipe follows)
¾ pound lean boneless pork, cut into ½-inch pieces
1½ pounds chicken breasts (about 3 half breasts), boned, skinned and cut into ½-inch pieces
2 tablespoons olive oil or salad oil
1 small onion, finely chopped
1 clove garlic, minced or pressed
½ green pepper, seeded and cut into thin strips
1 cup canned tomatoes
1 teaspoon salt
1 tablespoon finely chopped parsley

1. Prepare dough and let rise while preparing topping.

2. Brown pork and chicken pieces lightly in heated oil in a large heavy frying pan. Mix in onion, garlic and green pepper and cook, stirring occasionally, until vegetables are soft. Stir in tomatoes and salt. Bring to boiling, then cover, reduce heat and simmer 5 minutes. Uncover and cook, stirring occasionally, until most of the liquid is gone. Mix in parsley; remove from heat.

3. Punch dough down. Turn out onto lightly floured surface and roll into a 12-inch circle. Pat dough into a greased 12-inch pizza pan or shallow paella pan. Spread topping evenly over dough, leaving about a ½-inch margin at edge.

4. Bake in a 350°F/180°C oven until crust is golden brown, 40 to 45 minutes. Serve hot or at room temperature, cut into wedges.

Makes 4 to 6 servings.

Yeast Dough: In mixer bowl sprinkle 1 package active dry yeast over ⅓ cup warm water. Let stand a few minutes, then add 2 tablespoons olive oil or salad oil. Add 1 cup unsifted all-purpose flour and ½ teaspoon salt; mix to blend, then beat until dough is elastic and pulls away from sides of bowl. Stir in ¼ cup more flour to make a soft dough.

Measure additional ¼ cup flour; turn dough out onto board or pastry cloth floured with some of it. Knead until dough is smooth, adding more of the flour as necessary.

Place dough in greased bowl. Cover and let rise in warm place until doubled in bulk, 45 minutes to 1 hour.

Poppy-seed Fanciers Approve Of This Delicious Honey Cake

By Cecily Brownstone
AP Food Editor

An acquaintance of mine discovered a recipe for a delicious poppyseed cake in a book about spices and passed along the good news to me. Since then I've served the cake to some of the poppyseed fanciers among my friends and they've wanted to know how to make it. So here is my recipe.

The original recipe called for too small a baking pan, and I've changed that. It also called for a whole cup of poppy seed, but I favor a lesser amount. In addition, the recipe called for sifting the flour before measuring and then resifting with the leavening and salt. I find stirring instead of sifting produces as excellent a cake as did the original method. This is not the case in all cake recipes, but it's true in this one.

Poppy Seed Honey Cake

⅔ cup poppy seed
⅓ cup honey
¼ cup water
2½ cups flour, stir to aerate before measuring
1 teaspoon baking soda
1 teaspoon salt
1 cup butter
1½ cups sugar
4 eggs, separated
1 cup sour cream
1 teaspoon vanilla extract

Grease and flour a 10-inch angel cake pan.

In a small saucepan simmer together for 5 minutes, stirring often, the poppy seed, honey and water; cool.

On waxed paper thoroughly stir together the flour, baking soda and salt.

In a large bowl of an electric mixer cream butter and sugar; beat in poppy seed mixture.

At moderate speed, thoroughly beat in the egg yolks, one at a time; add sour cream and vanilla and beat until blended. At lowest speed, gradually beat in the flour mixture.

With a clean beater, in a small mixing bowl, beat egg whites until they form stiff straight peaks when the beater is slowly withdrawn; fold into batter. Turn into prepared pan.

Bake in 350-degree oven until a cake tester inserted in center comes out clean, about 55 minutes. Let stand on a wire rack for 5 minutes. With a small metal spatula, loosen edges and around tube and turn out onto rack; cool completely. Serve as is or spread top with powdered-sugar frosting, letting some of it drip down sides. Sprinkle top with poppy seed.

Broiled Filets

Sole, with only 80 calories per serving, is high in protein and minerals and low in fat. Try this Saucy Sole featuring broiled filets topped with a tangy sauce to keep them moist.

Cut 2 pounds sole filets into 6 portions. Place in a single layer on a greased baking platter and pour 2 tablespoons melted butter over fish. Combine ½ cup mayonnaise, 2 tablespoons chili sauce, ½ teaspoon celery salt, ½ teaspoon dry mustard, ½ teaspoon paprika and ½ teaspoon wine vinegar.

Broil fish about 4 inches from heat for 5 minutes. Spread mayonnaise mixture over fish and broil 3 to 5 minutes longer or until fish flakes. Makes 6 servings.

Dried Beef

You can make this colorful dish ahead, ready to reheat before serving. Tear sliced dried beef (5 ounces) into bite-size pieces. Cover with boiling water, let stand 3 to 5 minutes, then drain. Set aside.

Melt ¼ cup butter in frying pan over medium heat; add 1 medium-size onion, chopped, and saute until limp. Stir in 4 tablespoons flour and cook 1 minute. Slowly stir in 2 cups milk and cook, stirring until bubbly. Add ¼ teaspoon nutmeg, and salt and

Pumpkin Cake

In a large mixer bowl beat together 1 package spice cake mix, 2 eggs and ¼ cup LESS water than called for on cake mix package. Mix in ¾ cup canned pumpkin; stir in ¾ cup each nuts and dates, finely chopped.

Pour batter into greased tube pan. Bake at 350 degrees about 40 minutes or until cake tests done. Drizzle with a lemon-powdered sugar glaze.

FFLE MOLD IS SPLENDID WITH FLAVOR OF CANNED SWEET CHERRIES

Ensalade de Tomate
(Tomato Salad)

A salad of tomatoes and onions adds cool crispness to the spicy meal. Toss with olive oil and vinegar dressing laced with minced fresh or dried oregano.

Or, substitute a thermos of chilled gazpacho, the famous Spanish soup of chopped raw vegetables in a cold tomato broth. For a simple, but not authentic version, add chopped cucumber, onion, tomatoes and green peppers to cold canned tomato-vegetable cocktail juice in as generous amounts as you wish.

Pollo Frito
(Fried Chicken with Sherry and Garlic)

1. Fry flour-dusted, seasoned chicken pieces (3½ to 4-pound fryer) in olive oil.

2. Deglaze the pan with about ½ cup sherry and 1 or 2 cloves of garlic, finely minced. Pour this sauce over the crisp chicken and serve at room temperature.

Serves 4.

Emparadado de Jamon
(Egg-Dipped Fried Ham Sandwiches)

1. For each picnicker, make a ham sandwich and dip into well-beaten egg.

2. Fry in shallow olive oil until golden brown. Wrap in foil to keep warm, or serve cold.

Brazo de Gítano
(Arm of the Gypsy)

Top off your Spanish meal with strong hot coffee and Arm of the Gypsy (Brazo de Gítano).

1. Make a cake roll from your favorite sponge cake recipe baked in a jelly roll pan. Spread with freshly whipped sweetened cream or a flavored custard.

2. Roll as directed in the recipe, then decorate with additional whipped cream, chill.

Serves 6 to 8.

Note: If you're lucky enough to have a Spanish restaurant nearby, request the chef to prepare special picnic foods. Or apply this idea to Italian, German, Chinese or other specialized cuisines. Enroute to your outing, stop at the restaurant with your own food containers and a hamper for packing.

Bill Saylor stopped at El Greco to pick up the picnic prepared by Chef Pons. Foods are easy to pack into a neat set of modular, clear plastic containers with tight-fitting lids. They stack snugly inside most rectangular picnic baskets.

Inside a sunny courtyard, protected from the March winds, Bill serves *Empanada Gallega* to his wife, Jean, and their guest, who coincidentally is named Sherry.

Guide to Sherries from Spain

Naturally, Spanish food calls for sherry. Jerez de la Frontera in southwest Spain has been producing sherry for 3000 years. There are no vintage years to remember in selecting sherry as it is a blended wine of many harvests. Unlike other wines, sherry will keep almost indefinitely if corked tightly. Traditionally it is sipped from the tulip-shaped copa, but any glass is acceptable on a picnic.

Type	Character	Customarily Served
Manzanilla (man-than-ee-ya)	Very dry, light, pale golden	Chilled, before and with meals
Fino (feen-o)	Dry, light, pale golden	Chilled, before and with meals
Amontillado (ah-mon-tee-ya-do)	Moderately dry, medium body, golden	Room temperature or chilled anytime
Oloroso (o-lo-ro-so)	Gently sweet, full bodied, richly golden	At room temperature between and after meals
Cream	Sweet, heavy bodied, deep golden	At room temperature, after meals or over ice anytime

Latin Fiesta

For our South American fiesta, we turn to Brazil, where the cuisine assimilates Portuguese techniques and products, the seasonings of Africa, the indigenous fiery hot peppers and herbs, and cool, lush, tropical fruits.

Stage a fiesta on a warm summer day with colorful flags or windsocks marking your site. You must have music — a guitarist or a portable cassette recorder sounding Carioca rhythms through the trees.

Latin Fiesta for 12

Stuffed Cucumbers

Avocado Spread / Dark Bread or Crackers

Shrimp Salad Bahia

Picadillo

Fresh Tropical Fruits
Pineapple and Coconut Pudding

Spiced Brazilian Iced Coffee

(Recipe follows)

Think color when you plan a Latin fiesta. On our picnic table vivid hues are repeated in the woven tablecloth, baskets, paper plates, napkins, tropical flowers and fruits. From left to right the menu includes *Shrimp Salad Bahia, Avocado Spread, Picadillo* served from a dutch oven inside a basket, *Stuffed Cucumbers, Pineapple and Coconut Pudding* and *Spiced Brazilian Iced Coffee.*

Stuffed Cucumbers

A plateful of colorful cucumber circles is a cool way to start your fiesta.

6 medium-size cucumbers, rinsed

1½ teaspoons salt

3 packages cream cheese (8 oz. each), softened

¼ cup grated onion

½ cup finely chopped green pepper

2 teaspoons paprika

Freshly ground black pepper to taste

Spinach or lettuce leaves

Tomato wedges or pimento-stuffed olives (optional)

1. Cut ends from cucumbers, then score the skin lengthwise with fork. Cut each in half crosswise and remove seedy section with corer or paring knife. Rub 1 teaspoon salt inside cucumbers.

2. Combine cream cheese, onion, green pepper, paprika, black pepper and remaining salt; mix until well blended. Stuff cucumbers with the cheese mixture and wrap each half in foil. Refrigerate overnight.

3. At the picnic site, slice cucumbers crosswise in ¼-inch circles and arrange on a bed of spinach or lettuce leaves. If desired, garnish plate with tomato wedges or pimento-stuffed olives. Serves 12.

Shrimp Salad Bahia

Feel free to substitute cold chicken for the shrimp in this crunchy summer salad from Bahia.

3 pounds cooked shrimp, shelled and deveined

3 cups each celery and green or red peppers, sliced thinly

1½ cups chopped green onion

½ cup finely minced fresh coriander (cilantro)

Salt to taste

Lime Dressing (recipe follows)

Spinach leaves, rinsed and dried

8 green-tipped bananas

1½ cups unsweetened shredded coconut

1 cup salted peanuts

Avocado Spread

Spread on small pieces of dark bread or crackers, or use as a dip for chips or raw vegetables.

3 avocados, peeled and seeded

¾ cup freshly squeezed lime or lemon juice

4 tablespoons grated onion

½ cup blanched almonds, finely chopped

1. Combine shrimp, celery, peppers, onions, coriander and salt. Toss with Lime Dressing, cover and chill for several hours.

2. Just before serving time, mound shrimp salad on tray or in bowl lined with spinach leaves. Surround top of salad with peeled, sliced bananas. Sprinkle with coconut and peanuts.

Serves 12.

Lime Dressing: Combine 2½ teaspoons grated lime peel, ¾ cup freshly squeezed lime juice, 1¼ cups salad oil, 1 cup olive oil, 2½ teaspoons each crushed red chili pepper and ground cumin. Chill.

Makes about 3 cups dressing.

6 strips bacon, cooked until crisp and crumbled

Chili powder, salt, black and cayenne pepper to taste

1. In a mixing bowl, mash avocado pulp until smooth, then stir in lime or lemon juice and onion and blend well.

2. Add remaining ingredients and refrigerate.

Makes about 4 cups.

Picadillo (Spicy Beef Stew)

Usually served over rice, picadillo is a tasty picnic dish alone. Keep the dutch oven or casserole hot by wrapping in several thicknesses of newspaper, or serve at room temperature.

4 pounds lean beef chuck, cut into 1-inch cubes

1 tablespoon salt

Water

¼ cup olive oil

2 large onions, finely chopped

6 cloves garlic, minced or pressed

6 to 8 large tomatoes, peeled and chopped

3 red or green bell peppers, seeded and chopped

¾ cup small pimento-stuffed olives

¾ teaspoon ground cloves

1 teaspoon ground cumin

2 tablespoons red wine vinegar

1½ cups raisins

1 cup slivered almonds

1. Place beef in a 5 to 6-quart dutch oven or heavy casserole that can be used on range top. Add salt and enough water to just cover, then bring to boiling. Cover, reduce heat and simmer until beef is tender, about 1½ hours. Uncover and simmer until most of the liquid has evaporated, 1 hour or more.

2. While meat cooks, in a large heavy frying pan or dutch oven heat oil and sauté onions and garlic until soft and golden. Stir in tomatoes and cook 5 minutes; add peppers, olives, cloves, cumin and vinegar. Cover and simmer 15 minutes, then uncover and cook, stirring occasionally, until sauce is thick, about 30 minutes.

3. Combine tomato sauce and beef; stir in raisins and cook 10 minutes, stirring frequently. Mix in almonds.

Serves 12.

Pineapple and Coconut Pudding

2½ cups milk

2 cans (14 oz. each) sweetened condensed milk

4 egg yolks, beaten

½ cup cornstarch

1 teaspoon vanilla

2 9-inch sponge cake layers or pound cake loafs (purchased)

2 cups pineapple juice

½ cup light rum

2 large cans (20 oz. each) pineapple slices

1½ cups packaged grated coconut

2 cups whipping cream, beaten until stiff

1. Combine milks, egg yolks and cornstarch. Cook in the top of double boiler over hot water until thickened, stirring constantly, about 10 minutes. Then cook, without stirring, for 10 minutes. Remove custard from heat, add vanilla and cool.

2. Cut cake into small squares and layer in bottom of a 10 by 10-inch (or 3-quart) serving dish. Drain pineapple, reserving juice. Sprinkle with pineapple juice and rum, then cover with half the custard. Cut half of the pineapple slices into bite-size pieces and layer over the custard. Then layer with half of the coconut. Cover with remaining custard and top with whipped cream. Decorate with remaining coconut and pineapple rings.

Serves 12.

Spiced Brazilian Iced Coffee

1. Prepare 9 cups of very strong, dark roast coffee and pour, while still hot, over 12 whole cloves and 2 vanilla beans, split in half lengthwise. Cover and infuse for 1 hour. Strain; refrigerate.

2. At picnic, pour cold coffee and plenty of cream over crushed ice in tall glasses or plastic cups. Add sugar to taste; you may not want it as sweet as Brazilians prefer.

Makes 12 servings.

The exotic blending of shrimp and peppers marinated in lime with spinach, bananas, coconut and peanuts is a refreshing addition to the fiesta. For a simpler outing, prepare only the *Shrimp Salad Bahia*, rolls and your favorite beverage.

Swiss Fondue in the Snow

Several years back it seemed that everyone had discovered this perennial favorite from Switzerland, and fondue became the darling of the informal party. Perhaps the time has come for a revival of interest, this time translated to the outdoor dining scene. After all, what could be a more satisfying lunch on a short cross-country ski trip or snow hike than a pot of bubbly cheese fondue?

Everything you'll need can be tucked inside a daypack. Before leaving home, prepare all ingredients for the fondue and package in appropriate sized containers or plastic bags, and store inside the fondue pot. Don't forget 2 small cans of canned heat, long-handled dipping forks or bamboo skewers and a wooden spoon for stirring.

Daypack Checklist

☐ Fondue ingredients in small containers or plastic bags

☐ Bottle of dry white wine with ½ cup measure indicated (Open bottle, pour out ½ cup. Mark liquid line on bottle and replace wine. Recork securely.)

☐ Plastic glasses

☐ Paper plates

☐ Fondue forks or bamboo skewers

☐ Long wooden spoon

☐ 2 cans canned heat

☐ Fondue pot

Cheese Fondue

For success always select aged natural cheeses, not pasteurized kinds.

1 clove garlic, peeled and halved
1½ cups dry white wine
½ pound each **Emmenthal and Gruyère cheeses, grated**
1 teaspoon cornstarch
3 tablespoons kirsch
Nutmeg or white pepper to taste
1 loaf French or Italian bread, cubed into bite-size pieces
1 apple, sliced and cored

1. Rub inside of fondue pot with garlic. Pour wine into fondue pot over moderate high heat and bring to a simmer. Slowly add cheese, a little at a time. Stir constantly, allowing each addition to melt before adding more. (This can take 30 minutes; you may need the second can of fuel.) Do not allow to boil.

2. When smooth, add the cornstarch which has been blended into the kirsch, stirring vigorously. Add seasonings and reduce heat to low. Fondue is now ready to eat and will continue to thicken over low heat.

To eat, dip bread or apple slice on long-handled forks into the hot fondue. For additional taste sensation, take along extra kirsch and dip bread or apples before dipping into fondue.

Serves 2 to 4.

Fondue for 2

Cheese Fondue

French or Italian Bread

Carrot and Celery Sticks / Sour Pickles

Swiss Chocolate Bars

Dry White Wine

(Recipe above)

Ingredients for Swiss fondue can be packed inside plastic bags, then stuffed into the fondue pot along with other items on the menu and then into a daypack. We suggest a lightweight pot and premeasured amounts of wine and kirsch in small containers for easy carrying.

Middle East Feast

The finger foods of the Armenians, Greeks, Lebanese, Israelis and Turks combine into a completely vegetarian meal that's perfectly portable. You'll need a low table just off the ground so guests can sit within easy reach of the foods. Saw off wooden legs of a card-table to make an 8-inch high food platform, or rest a picnic table with legs folded up on four large stones. Throw a large cotton bedspread over the table, letting it extend onto the ground all around. Arrange large pillows for caftan-clad guests.

Encourage guests to eat with their fingers. Start with **dolmas**, grape leaves stuffed with seasoned rice, a treat common to the entire Mediterranean. Then everyone builds his own "sandwich" inside **pita** bread, or on top of crispy Armenian cracker bread, **lavash**. To eat the meal with **pita** bread, cut or pull a round

in half, across the diameter, gently separating to form a pocket. Layer **hummus, tabbuli** and any of the chosen condiments. Or stack up the same foods on pieces of the cracker bread.

If you have a delicatessen nearby that offers Middle Eastern foods, you're in luck. Markets that stock specialty foods will also have some of the menu items. (Imported **dolmas** in cans are surprisingly tasty.) If there isn't a source of such delicacies where you live, plan to make some substitutions if you don't want to cook from scratch. Any large crispy cracker can be used in lieu of **lavash**. If **pita** can't be found, do take the time to make your own; there's really no substitute. Many bakeries carry some Greek pastries, at least **baklava**. (Homemade pastries for our picnic came from a Greek Orthodox church food festival.) Or, offer a tangy lemon pound or yogurt cake. Should pomegranate juice prove hard to find, substitute pink lemonade or other fruit based summer drink. Middle Easterners are also big fans of bottled waters.

If you have a source of heat available at the picnic site, prepare Turkish coffee after the meal, or offer very strong black coffee from a thermos.

For our middle eastern picnic we found a gravelly spot alongside a lake that had the right atmosphere. The low table is a folded metal picnic table set on four rocks. The cloth is a woven Mediterranean bedspread extended onto the ground to also provide seating. You might ask your guests to wear caftans, but don't expect everyone to be able to cooperate. Min Yee, second from right, joined Chris, Alan, Candy and Lenny at the last minute.

Tabbuli (Cracked Wheat Salad)

Some versions of this ancient dish call for more bulgur or cracked wheat. This tasty concoction uses a lot of parsley, resulting in a lighter salad.

- **2 bunches parsley, chopped extremely fine, or minced in food processor with steel knife (about 1½ cups, chopped)**
- **½ cup finely minced green onions**
- **3 medium tomatoes, peeled and finely diced**
- **½ cup bulgur (cracked wheat), washed and drained**
- **¼ cup freshly squeezed lemon juice, or more to taste**
- **¼ cup olive oil**
- **Salt and freshly ground pepper to taste**

1. Combine all ingredients, correct seasonings.

2. Refrigerate overnight for bulgur to absorb moisture.

Serves 6.

Turkish Coffee

If powdered Turkish coffee is not available, substitute any strong roast coffee in pulverized form.

1. Combine 2 cups cold water and ¼ cup granulated sugar in a specially shaped Turkish brass coffee pot or small saucepan. Heat to boiling over high heat, stirring just until sugar is dissolved.

2. Add 1 teaspoon ground cardamom and ¼ cup pulverized Turkish or dark roast coffee. Stir constantly until thick and smooth, about 1 minute. Heat until thick foam rises, about 30 seconds. Remove from heat and spoon foam into each of 6 demitasse (or the smallest cups you have).

3. Bring coffee to boiling twice more, removing pot each time foam rises and dividing evenly among the cups. Pour remaining coffee into each cup. Let stand 2 minutes before drinking.

Makes 6 servings.

Hummus Bi Tahini (Garbanzo Purée)

Canned garbanzo beans simplify the preparation of this high protein spread or dip. You may want to double the recipe to allow large portions. Any left over keeps well in the refrigerator.

- **2 cans (1 lb. each) garbanzo beans**
- **4 cloves garlic, minced**
- **1 cup (8 oz.) tahini, canned (see note)**
- **1 cup water (use part garbanzo liquid)**
- **½ cup freshly squeezed lemon juice**
- **¼ cup olive oil**
- **Salt to taste**
- **Olive oil**
- **Mint sprigs, paprika or pomegranate seeds for garnish**

1. In saucepan heat garbanzos to boiling point. Cool slightly and place in blender or food processor with a little liquid, reserving remaining liquid. Purée until smooth, then add garlic, tahini, reserved garbanzo liquid and water to make 1 cup, lemon juice, oil and salt. Add a bit more water, if necessary, to make a creamy consistency. Correct seasonings.

2. To serve, spread on a plate or in bowl. Drizzle with olive oil and garnish with mint leaves, paprika and pomegranate seeds as desired. Serve with pita or lavash.

Makes about 4 cups.

Note: Tahini is a thick paste of sesame seeds available in gourmet markets, Greek or other Middle Eastern shops.

Pomegranate Cooler

1. At home combine 1 quart each cold bottled sweet pomegranate juice and rosé wine in chilled thermos jug.

2. At the picnic site add 1 quart cold club soda. If you prefer nonalcoholic beverages, simply omit the wine. Add a wedge of lemon to each glass. Serves 6.

Lavash (Armenian Cracker Bread)

Lavash keeps about two weeks when stored in a dry place.

- **1 package active dry yeast**
- **¼ cup warm water**
- **6 cups unsifted all-purpose flour, approximately**
- **2 teaspoons salt**
- **2 cups milk, scalded and cooled to lukewarm**
- **1 tablespoon sugar**
- **½ cup butter or margarine, melted and cooled to lukewarm**
- **Sesame seeds (optional)**

1. Soften yeast in water. Mix 5½ cups of the flour and salt in large bowl and make a well at the center. Pour in yeast mixture, milk, sugar and butter, mixing well.

2. Turn dough onto a well-floured board or onto a pastry cloth floured with some of the remaining ½ cup flour and knead until smooth and elastic. Add more flour, if necessary. Place in greased bowl, turning dough to coat on all sides. Cover and let rise until doubled, about 1 hour and 15 minutes.

3. Punch dough down and divide into 4 equal portions. Working with 1 portion at a time, roll each on a floured surface into a thin round 15 to 17 inches in diameter. Place on ungreased 15 to 17-inch pizza pan or round baking sheet; sprinkle lightly with sesame seeds, if you wish.

4. Bake on lowest rack of a 350°F/180°C oven until crisp and lightly browned, 20 to 25 minutes. Cool before storing. Break into irregular pieces to serve.

Makes 4 large round flat breads.

Pita (Arab Pocket Bread)

Pita is excellent for stuffing with any of your favorite fillings for dripless sandwiches. Pocket bread keeps well when stored airtight in the refrigerator or freezer.

- **1 package active dry yeast**
- **1 tablespoon sugar**
- **3 cups warm water**
- **1 tablespoon each salt and oil**
- **9 cups all-purpose flour**

1. Add yeast and sugar to water in a large bowl; let stand 5 minutes. Mix in salt and oil. Gradually mix in flour, first beating with mixer or a heavy wooden spoon, then mixing the dough with your hands until it holds together.

2. Turn dough onto a well-floured board or pastry cloth and shape into a long rounded loaf. Divide in half, then cut each half into 10 equal pieces.

3. Keeping surface and hands well-floured, knead each piece until smooth and elastic. Place, smooth sides up, on a dry cloth. Cover with damp cloth and let rise 1 to 1½ hours, until puffy.

4. Place each piece on board, flatten and roll from center in each direction to form a 6-inch round. Place ½ inch apart on dry cloth, then cover with another dry cloth, topped with a damp cloth. Cover with plastic wrap and let rise until slightly puffed, about 1 hour.

5. Carefully place pitas, a few at a time, ½ inch apart on ungreased baking sheet. Place oven rack at lowest position and bake in 500°F/260°C oven until breads are puffed and bottoms browned slightly, about 5 minutes. Immediately set oven to broil and reposition baking sheet 4 inches below broiler unit. Broil until tops are lightly browned, 1 to 2 minutes. (If you have two ovens, set one at 500°F/260°C and the other at broil.) Cool pitas on a towel, then flatten gently.

Makes 20 individual breads.

Russian Easter Brunch

Old Russia celebrated magnificently. Today there are still Russians in the USSR and scattered abroad who cling to the time honored foods which herald the beginning of spring.

During the Easter holidays pack a basket with Russian delicacies and find a beautiful meadow with wildflowers or a knoll covered with new green grass. After brunch, involve the entire group, adults too, in an old fashioned egg roll or hunt.

Pirozhkis are meat or vegetable filled Russian pastries. They're available in many types of delicatessens across the country.

The rich Russian coffee cake, **kulich**, usually is served with an even richer, creamy dessert, **paskha**. Both take some effort to prepare, but one taste makes it all worthwhile.

Russian Easter Feast for 8

Cold Beet Borshch

Pirozhki

Baked Ham, Roast Leg of Lamb, or Smoked Fish

Stuffed Eggs / Vegetable Salad

Kulich / Paskha

Hot Tea or Coffee / Chilled Orange Juice

(Recipe follows)

Cold Beet Borshch

Here's a very simple version of Russia's most famous soup. Prepare a day or two ahead and refrigerate.

- ½ medium-size onion, chopped
- Oil
- 1 clove garlic, minced
- 1 jar (32 oz.) borshch with beets
- 1 cup canned chicken broth
- 1 large potato, diced
- 2 carrots, diced
- ½ cup canned tomatoes, broken up
- ½ cup shredded cabbage, about ¼ small head
- ½ cup water
- 1 tablespoon chopped parsley
- Salt and pepper to taste
- 1½ to 2 tablespoons lemon juice
- Sour cream

1. Brown onions and garlic in hot oil in 2-quart heavy saucepan. Add borshch, chicken broth, potatoes, carrots and tomatoes; cover and simmer ½ hour.

2. Add cabbage, water and parsley, cover and simmer at least ½ hour longer, or until cabbage is very tender. Add salt and pepper to taste.

3. Cool and refrigerate. Pour into chilled thermos, add 1½ to 2 tablespoons lemon juice. At picnic, serve in mugs with dollops of sour cream.

Makes 8 half cup servings.

Vegetable Salad

1. Fresh vegetables taste best, although frozen or canned may be used. Cook separately just until tender 1 cup each peas and diced carrots and 2 cups diced beets. Drain well and chill.

2. Combine with 1 cup sour cream and salt to taste.

Makes 8 half-cup servings.

An egg hunt followed by an egg roll on a sloping lawn introduces excitement to any Easter picnic.

Kulich (Easter Coffee Cake)

- ½ teaspoon saffron
- ⅓ cup dark rum
- ¾ cup raisins
- ½ cup mixed candied fruits
- 1 cup toasted blanched almonds, chopped (see note)
- 5 to 6 cups unsifted all-purpose flour
- 3 packages active dry yeast
- ¼ cup milk, scalded, then cooled
- 1 cup plus 2 tablespoons light brown sugar
- ¾ cup sweet butter, at room temperature
- 1 teaspoon almond extract
- ½ teaspoon anise extract
- 3 eggs
- 1 cup whipping cream, scalded, then cooled
- Egg White Frosting (recipe follows)
- Colored sprinkles or sliced almonds, for decoration

1. Soak saffron in rum at least 1 hour. Mix raisins, candied fruits, almonds and 1 cup of the flour; set aside.

2. Soften yeast in milk with 2 tablespoons of the brown sugar; let stand until bubbly, about 10 minutes.

3. Cream butter and remaining 1 cup brown sugar in large bowl of electric mixer until fluffy. Beat in almond and anise extracts, then beat in eggs, one at a time, beating until smooth after each addition. Beat in 2 cups of the flour until smooth. Blend in rum-saffron mixture, then cream. Blend in yeast mixture. Gradually add 2 cups of the remaining flour, beating until smooth and elastic. Mix in about ½ cup more flour to make a soft dough.

4. Place dough in greased bowl, turning to coat all sides. Cover with plastic wrap and a towel; let rise in warm place until doubled in bulk, about 3 hours.

5. Punch dough down, turn onto floured board or pastry cloth and knead in fruit and flour mixture.

6. Cut waxed paper circles to fit bottoms of two 2-pound coffee cans. Grease sides and bottoms generously, line with waxed paper and grease waxed paper. Divide dough evenly into the 2 coffee cans (dough should half fill them). Smooth tops and cover with waxed paper. Let rise in warm place until dough rises almost to tops of cans, 1½ to 2 hours. Remove paper.

7. Bake in a 375°F/190°C oven 15 minutes; lower heat to 325°F/160°C and bake until skewer inserted in center of each comes out clean, about 40 minutes. If tops become too brown near end of baking time, cover breads lightly with foil.

8. Cool bread in cans on wire rack 10 minutes; then turn out onto rack to complete cooling. When cool, frost tops with Egg White Icing, letting some drizzle down sides. Decorate with colored sprinkles or sliced almonds.

9. To serve, cut ½-inch slices from bottoms of loaves; cut slices in halves. Place uncut decorated tops in center of serving plate; surround with halved slices.

Makes 2 loaves.

Egg White Icing:
Beat 1 egg white in small mixer bowl on high speed until soft peaks form. Beat in 2 cups powdered sugar gradually at medium speed; beat in ½ teaspoon vanilla. Stir in 2 to 3 tablespoons water, a few drops at a time, until frosting is of spreading consistency.

Note: To toast almonds, spread in shallow pan and bake in 350°F/180°C oven 8 to 10 minutes, until lightly browned.

Paskha

This is a lovely molded dessert, as rich and elegant as the court of old Russia. Tall molds are available from gourmet cooking stores, but a new, washed 6-inch clay flowerpot works well.

2 pounds cream cheese, softened
1 cup sweet butter, softened
5 egg yolks
2 cups powdered sugar
1 envelope unflavored gelatin
2 tablespoons cold water
1 tablespoon vanilla
1 cup whipping cream
2 tablespoons kirsch
¾ cup toasted slivered almonds (see note)
Fresh whole strawberries and mixed candied fruits, for garnish

1. Beat cheese and butter at low speed with electric mixer until well blended. Add egg yolks, one at a time, beating well after each addition. Gradually beat in sugar.

2. Soften gelatin in cold water, then dissolve over simmering water; blend into cheese mixture. Add vanilla. Whip cream with kirsch until stiff; fold into cheese mixture. Fold in almonds.

3. Line a washed, dried, chilled 6-inch flower pot or 2-quart glass container with cheesecloth that has been rinsed in cold water and well wrung. Spoon mixture into pot, filling to the top. Place pot in a shallow pan. Cover with plastic wrap and refrigerate at least overnight, or up to 4 to 5 days. Transport to picnic still in pot.

4. Loosen edges carefully with flexible spatula.

Carry along a basket of traditional Russian spring-time treats—tall coffee cake, *kulich*, that is sliced and spread with cone-shaped, creamy *paskha*. Or course, add spring flowers and Easter eggs. These were hand-painted in Russia.

Position plate over the pot, invert quickly and gently remove pot. Carefully remove cheesecloth. Surround with strawberries and decorate with candied fruit. Tradition calls for the letters XB on the side, the Orthodox symbol meaning "Christ is risen." Cut into thin wedges to spread on half-rounds of kulich.

Makes 12 to 15 servings.

Note: To toast almonds, spread in shallow pan and bake in 350°F/180°C oven until lightly browned, 6 to 8 minutes.

Alternative Menu Suggestions

● Instead of **pirozhkis**, any meat-filled turnover can be served with the borshch. Check delicatessens, frozen food cases or follow the recipe for Chicken Turnovers on page 35, substituting ground beef, mushrooms, or any desired filling.

● Buttery sweet rolls are a simple alternative to **kulich** and strawberries in sour cream with a sprinkle of brown sugar can substitute for **paskha**.

Scandinavian Smörgåsbord

Each Scandinavian country specializes in foods that lend themselves well to picnic fare. Denmark proudly creates butter-rich open sandwiches, **smørrebrød**, topped with an array of cold meats and fish; Norwegian cooks work wonders with dill-poached salmon and cucumber salad; in Sweden herring dishes and marinated fish are the specialties; and in Finland **akvavit** or **schnapps**, an icy cold vodka flavored with caraway seeds or other herbs and spices, is consumed in great quantities with smoked meats. One feature shared in common is the "cold table," known the world over by the Swedish name "smörgåsbord."

Originally created to serve large numbers of people, the smörgåsbord features a wide variety of fish dishes, hot and cold meats, numerous salads, pickles, cheeses, fresh fruits, breads and crackers with sweet butter. The list is endless. We heartily recommend a smörgåsbord not only for a large hungry group, but also a scaled-down party.

If possible, set your picnic table with crisp modern, simple Scandinavian designed linens and tableware. Provide plenty of plates, perhaps paper, because custom dictates that these be changed frequently to avoid mixing flavors.

Feature plenty of cold foods, but be sure to add a few hot dishes kept warm in chafing dishes. Or grill fresh fish on the hibachi as the hosts did at our Finnish picnic.

We do not provide recipes for this picnic — most food items can be bought ready-made from delicatessen cases, packaged or canned from grocery shelves.

You'll find several herring, shrimp, and other appropriate recipes in the Ortho book, **All About Pickling**. Any complete cookbook will offer recipes for Swedish meatballs, red cabbage and other hot dishes. Desserts are usually not served, but add buttery sugar cookies with the hot coffee to satisfy the American sweet tooth.

A smörgåsbord is designed to provide many different tastes for different folks. No one is expected to eat his way through it all, although many of us will try!

Above: A smörgåsbord doesn't always have to be set up for a large group. We staged a typical "cold table" for a family outing. Open-faced Danish *smørrebrød* have a variety of garnishes. A chafing dish keeps Swedish meatballs hot to contrast with the cold dishes. Both homemade and delicatessen dishes are easy to pack in sleek modular storage boxes.

Right: This assortment of bread was photographed in Finland, but check your bakery and grocery shelves for substitute rich, dark breads and imported Scandinavian crackers and flatbreads.

Smörgåsbord for 25 or More

(Select several dishes from each category.
Serve in bite-size portions where possible;
thinly slice meat and fish.)

Cold Dishes

Marinated Herring (1 quart)

Herring Salad (1 quart)

Herring in Sour Cream (1 quart)

Lumpfish Caviar (1 pound)

Sardines (4 cans)

Smoked Salmon (1 pound)

Boiled Shrimp (2 pounds)

Marinated Shrimp (2 pounds)

Crayfish or Lobster (2 pounds)

Liver Pâté (1½ pounds)

Steak Tartare (2 pounds)

Roast Beef (1 pound)

Smoked Ham (1 pound)

Hard Cooked Eggs (25)

Pickled Beets (1½ quarts)

Cucumber Salad (1½ quarts)

Tomato Salad (1½ quarts)

Green Pea Salad (1½ quarts)

Carrot and Raisin Salad (1 pound)

Coleslaw (3 pounds)

Potato Salad (5 pounds)

Tossed Green Salad (1 large)

Pickled Peaches (25)

Spiced Plums (25)

Scandinavian Cheeses

(2 pounds total)

Norwegian Jarlsberg

Finnish Emmenthal

Danish Blue or Danbo

Swedish Herrgård

Assorted Scandinavian Bread and Crackers

Fresh Fruits (25, a variety)

Fruit in Sour Cream (1½ quarts)

Hot Dishes

Swedish Meatballs (50)

Roast Pork with Sautéed Apples (4 pounds)

Red Cabbage (1½ quarts)

Grilled Ground Beef Patties (25 small) with
Sautéed Onion Rings

Grilled Flounder or other fish (2 large)

Beverages

Akvavit or Vodka (frozen in
ice block, see page 105)

Cold Beer

White Wine

Apple Juice

Hot Coffee

Our Finnish hosts prepared an outdoor smörgåsbord featuring a grilled fish as the hot dish. Marimekko fabrics covered the picnic tables set with simple Scandinavian-designed tableware. Other tables nearby held a wide assortment of typical Finnish cold dishes.

Portable Philippine Meal

Picnicking is a year-round pastime in the Philippines. Favorite foods are taken to parks and beaches and consumed with icy cold beer or sodas. There's a definite tropical sweetness to Philippine cuisine. Many dishes, including breads, are prepared with coconut milk, and freshly grated coconut is sprinkled on other foods. Luscious tropical fruits are served throughout the meal — pineapples, mangoes, papayas, guavas and bananas.

In our portable Philippine meal, everything can be made ahead and served at room temperature. If you choose, **lumpia** (fried egg rolls) and **adobo** (pork and chicken casserole) can be reheated just before leaving for the picnic, wrapped well and served while still warm.

The use of frozen **lumpia** wrappers, now available in many metropolitan markets, simplifies preparation. If unavailable, make the egg pancakes (recipe follows) in a crêpe pan or 8-inch, non-stick skillet.

The breads of the islands are usually prepared in the bakery rather than at home. We bought assorted Philippine sweet breads at a local San Francisco grocery, but in lieu of authentic breads, substitute any good, sweet yeast rolls.

Philippine Picnic for 6
Adobo (Pork and Chicken Casserole)

Lumpia (Fried Egg Roll)

Pickled Red Eggs

Philippine Breads:
Pan de Sal, Pan de Leche
Fresh Tropical Fruits
Cold Beer or Soda

(Recipe follows)

Below: Crisp, golden-fried *lumpia* make excellent picnic fare to be eaten out of hand. (Preparation is especially easy if you have access to frozen wrappers.) *Lumpia* are best eaten still warm, but remain tasty when cold. Make in quantity and freeze; thaw a few at a time and refry them quickly to heat through just before your outing.

Adobo (Pork and Chicken Casserole)

Traditionally, adobo is served with rice flour bread, pan de sal, or with steamed rice taken to the picnic wrapped in banana leaves.

4 pounds boneless pork, cubed	
1 cup vinegar	
1 cup soy sauce	
¼ tablespoon black pepper	
½ teaspoon salt	
1 clove garlic, minced	
1 bay leaf	
1 chicken (3 to 4 lbs.), cooked, boned, cut into bite-size pieces	
½ pound mushrooms	

1. In a large heavy saucepan combine all ingredients except chicken and mushrooms. Cook, covered, over low heat until pork is tender, about 20 to 30 minutes.

2. Add chicken pieces and simmer 20 minutes longer. Then stir in whole mushrooms and cook 5 minutes or until tender. Mixture will be souplike.

Serves 6.

Pickled Red Eggs

Duck eggs are favored in the Philippines, but as this may require some forethought, substitute chicken eggs.

1. Place 12 eggs in shells in water sufficient to cover. Pour 1 cup rock salt into the water as a preservative and keep eggs immersed, and refrigerated, for 30 days.

2. After the 30th day, hardcook the eggs, then dye with beet juice or red food coloring as you would Easter eggs.

Red eggs, diced and mixed with chopped fresh tomatoes are good with rice.

Right: A large palm leaf fan is the unusual table for a Philippine picnic prepared by Terry Robinson, right. She agreed to pass along three recipes that are easy: *adobo* (in the center of the table) is a casserole of pork and chicken that's good hot or cold; colorful pickled red eggs; and *lumpia*, in the basket.

Lumpia
(Fried Egg Rolls)

1 medium onion, finely chopped	
1 clove garlic, minced or pressed	
1 tablespoon salad oil	
½ pound ground pork, crumbled	
3 medium carrots, about ½ pound, diced	
3 medium potatoes, about 1½ pounds, diced	
½ pound green beans, sliced diagonally into ½-inch pieces	
Half of a small green cabbage, finely chopped	
1½ teaspoons salt	
⅛ teaspoon pepper	
50 lumpia wrappers, thawed if frozen, or Egg Pancake Wrappers (recipe follows)	
Salad oil for frying	

1. Sauté onion and garlic in the 1 tablespoon oil in a large, deep frying pan or Dutch oven until soft. Mix in pork, carrots, potatoes and beans and cook over medium heat until potatoes are tender, stirring frequently, about 30 minutes. Remove from heat and mix in cabbage, salt and pepper.

2. Place about 2 tablespoons of the filling mixture in the center of each wrapper, spreading toward sides. Fold the lower flap along the length of the filling, then fold in sides and roll up; moisten top edge with a bit of water to seal.

3. Fry, 5 or 6 at a time, in shallow oil until golden. Drain on paper towels. Wrap in foil and serve warm, if possible.

Makes about 50.

Egg Pancake Wrappers:

1. Beat 8 eggs with 4 teaspoons salt. Mix in 4 cups water, then gradually beat in 4 cups unsifted all-purpose flour until smooth. If mixture is lumpy, whirl about a third at a time in blender until smooth. Refrigerate batter about 1 hour before making crêpes.

2. Grease a 6-inch crêpe pan and heat over moderately high heat. Pour in just enough batter to coat bottom lightly, swirling to coat evenly. Cook until bubbly and set, then turn and cook briefly on other side. Remove and stack while cooking remaining crêpes until all batter is used. Crêpes may be made ahead and frozen until ready to fill.

Makes about 50 six-inch crêpes.

Sara Slavin enjoys a crisp *lumpia*. For a quick getaway picnic all you really need are these crisp egg rolls, a favorite beverage and fresh fruit.

Any Time, Any Place

The emphasis in this chapter is on **where** and **when,** featuring the picnic site rather than the food. In preparing and photographing these picnics we tried to include all kinds of locations, from a hot tub to a zoo, a park bench to a table made of snow.

Agreed, the very word "picnic" conjures up visions of lazy, sunny summer afternoons in a meadow, by a stream, under a tree. But to qualify as a true picnicker, put those overworked images to rest. The world of portable feasting really is not confined by many limitations — the weather, the season, time of day or locale. Almost any pleasant spot can be a picnic site if you are in the right frame of mind.

Some of the finest picnic experiences can take place in the snow, on a rooftop high above the city, under a make-do shelter during a sudden spring shower, after a chilly hike in a spectacular autumn forest — or drifting high above it all in a hot air balloon! Consider the heady experience of breakfasting on the beach at dawn, or a mountain supper in the long, last shafts of the sunset.

Most recreations can include a picnic of some sort — tote along a few favorite foods to sports events, the movies, outdoor concerts, or to pass the time if you're waiting somewhere in an hours-long line. You can turn traveling into one big pack-your-own picnic instead of eating airline meals or stopping at roadside restaurants.

And, of course, picnics don't have to be outdoors. With the good company of a stack of crackers, cheese and cocoa, stretch out by a roaring fire. Spread a holiday supper for friends under the Christmas tree, or serve guests inside a greenhouse or a cozy, sunwarmed corner of the porch on a winter day.

Always be prepared for spur-of-the-moment outings. Keep your pantry stocked with getaway foods. Impromptu picnicking requires storing a few of the basics in the trunk of the car or in an everyday hamper in the hall closet: a blanket or tablecloth, can opener, corkscrew, a knife, plastic or paper tableware, some napkins. Get set for a picnic any time, any place.

In some of the picnics that follow, specific menus are not given, but there are many food suggestions to choose from that will fit the place, time and theme.

To prove our point that picnics can be fun any time, any place, we went to two extremes. Opposite: Cross country skiers Judith, Brian and Nancy quickly dug a table and banquette in the snow for an unconventional outdoor dining room. A waterproof, fold-up kit (see page 97 for directions) held all the plates and doubled as the tablecloth. Food was easy to carry inside a day pack; even the thermos of hot pea soup was not especially awkward. Above: In Finland, we snapped a picnic arranged inside a family sauna, the perfect way to end a day.

Christmas Picnicking

Christmastime provides at least two occasions to stage picnics, indoors and out. If you live near a place where you can select and cut your own tree, carry along a thermos of hot soup and some hearty sandwiches to help take the chill off the December day.

Then on Christmas Eve, after the tree is decorated, presents wrapped, children tucked away and all the last minute scurrying ended, settle down and enjoy a quiet picnic with family and close friends. Spread a quilt on the floor and put out good foods that have been readied a day or so in advance. Steaming oyster stew can be concocted in a matter of minutes while the quiche and cranberry tea are heating. Roll in your feast on a shiny red wagon buffet. (If a wagon doesn't figure in your gift plans, borrow one.) Holiday music and the shimmer of candles mellow the mood, too. Relax and enjoy a leisurely meal, planned as light contrast to the overindulgence that's apt to follow on Christmas Day.

Make a quiche from your favorite recipe or purchase one from a bakery and reheat at the last minute. The yule log, **Bûche de Noël**, can be ordered from a pastry shop for convenience, or substitute any dessert favorite. Sparkling apple cider has all the bubble and elegance of champagne, but no alcohol.

Under-the-Tree Picnic for 4
Oyster Stew

Quiche

Crudités with Green Mayonnaise

Bread Sticks

Venetian Glacéed Oranges

Bûche de Noël (Yule Log)

Chilled Sparkling Apple Cider

Hot Cranberry Tea

(Recipe follows)

A shiny red wagon is a perfect close-to-the-floor buffet for a late evening picnic supper underneath the Christmas tree. Easy to prepare, the meal is served on an appliqued and embroidered quilt. The tree is loaded with fanciful toys from the collection of animator Lenny Meyer, seated on the left.

Oyster Stew

No soup could be easier to prepare or more delicious on a winter evening. Our version calls for more oysters than most and is for true oyster lovers.

1 quart shelled oysters with their liquid, or four 8-ounce cans of small oysters
1½ cups milk
½ cup whipping cream
¼ cup butter
⅛ teaspoon white pepper
Salt to taste
Minced parsley (garnish)

1. Combine oysters and their liquid, milk, cream, butter and pepper in top of a double boiler set over, but not touching, the boiling water.

2. Stew is ready to serve when milk is hot, butter has melted and oysters float. Taste and add salt, if necessary. Garnish with a sprinkling of parsley.

Serves 4.

Note: If using large Pacific oysters, cut them into bite-size pieces before cooking.

Venetian Glacéed Oranges

A festive Italian tradition turns fresh oranges into something very special.

4 large navel oranges
1 cup sugar
½ cup water
¼ cup kirsch

1. Remove peel and white membrane from oranges. Sliver 2 tablespoons orange peel and combine with sugar and water in small saucepan.

2. Without stirring, cook syrup over moderate heat for 5 to 8 minutes, until slightly thickened.

3. Place oranges in thickened syrup and cook gently for 5 minutes, basting constantly. Remove from heat; add kirsch.

4. Chill oranges, occasionally spooning over syrup. At serving time, drain briefly on wire racks. Provide guests with forks and sharp fruit knives.

Serves 4.

Crudités with Green Mayonnaise

1. Prepare raw vegetables the day before. Wash and cut into chunky pieces seasonal fresh vegetables — cauliflower, broccoli, zucchini, mushrooms, tiny carrots. Store in airtight containers and chill until serving time.

2. Arrange on a plate or in a basket with a bowl of Green Mayonnaise nearby for dipping.

Green Mayonnaise: To blender or food processor bowl add 2 egg yolks (room temperature), 1 tablespoon Dijon-style mustard, 2 tablespoons lemon juice, 1 tablespoon white wine vinegar, 1 teaspoon each salt and sugar and blend for a few seconds. With motor running, gradually add 1 cup safflower oil in a slow steady stream.

Add 12 small sprigs watercress, 10 spinach leaves, several sprigs chervil, tarragon, parsley or other fresh herbs (if available) and 2 tablespoons chopped capers. Blend thoroughly and pour into serving bowl.

Makes 1½ cups.

Hot Cranberry Tea

This recipe makes a large quantity: keep refrigerated or frozen in small batches and heat only amount you want to serve. (It's also good with ice for warm-weather picnics.)

1½ quarts cranberry juice cocktail
1 cup sugar
3 quarts water
12 whole cloves
1 stick cinnamon
1 large can (12 oz.) frozen orange juice concentrate with 1 juice can water
1 large can (12 oz.) frozen lemon juice with 1 juice can water
2 cups pineapple juice

1. Combine cranberry juice, sugar and 1 quart of the water with cloves and cinnamon.

2. Simmer 15 minutes, then add remaining ingredients and heat thoroughly. Do not boil.

Makes about 6½ quarts.

Under the tree is a gift hamper packed with cheeses, crackers, pâté, mustard, sausages and sweets. Put together your own collection of treats for holiday giving to anyone who loves picnicking. For a gift on a grand scale, fit out a basket, as shown on page 95.

Pick Up and Go – Inner-City Style

City dwellers have an infinite number of picnic possibilities without leaving town. Usually, there are parks of every size and often zoo and museum picnic areas. Don't overlook botanical gardens or a quiet suburban oasis at the end of a city bus route.

Inventive city picnickers will look to the rooftops for great escapes — penthouse gardens, apartment balconies or public-access roofs atop highrise complexes.

Many cities have financial districts that are virtual ghost towns on weekends and holidays. There you'll often find open areas creatively designed for use by office workers during the week. Take advantage of these when you can have them almost to yourself. Public monument areas and pocket parks in normally crowded downtown shopping sections offer excellent backdrops for Sunday picnicking. Or take the Sunday paper, along with your breakfast, to a nearby patch of sunlight or greenery. Water-edged cities such as New York, Miami, Seattle and San Francisco offer cruises, the perfect way to enjoy a weekend picnic brunch and see your city from a new point of view.

Encourage friends living in huge city lofts and studios to throw portable banquets on cold or rainy days. Know someone with an art gallery or showroom? These are great after-hours spots for a big, extravagant midwinter picnic held indoors.

Instead of the usual weekday lunch break, relax in a nearby park with a splendid little basket of snacks just for you, or to share with a special friend. It's a quick refreshment before the afternoon's work.

If a movie theater has concession stands and allows snacking, chances are you can get away with carrying in a few treats of your own, especially vital for double features. But please pack everything in containers that open quietly. Movie fare should be simple, quiet and not odoriferous. Don't carry in anything that will infuriate or tempt those around you!

Many neighborhood groups stage block parties: pot luck picnics set up in the middle of a closed street. If you don't have such events where you live, organize one and get to know your neighbors. Check with police for permission to use the street.

A picnic connoisseur we know, when feeling extravagant, will rent a limousine for a couple of hours. After a few stops at favorite markets, bakeries and delicatessens, he enjoys his meal in transit while being chauffered around the city.

All you need to find great picnicking in the midst of the city is imagination, and sometimes more than a little nerve.

Judith Whipple and friend Steve Reiss go to the movies prepared to picnic. The woven bag carries apples, oranges, cheese sticks, caramel popcorn and hard candies in containers that open quietly.

Above: A solitary picnic on a park bench with a good book can be a welcome retreat from the bustling city. Treat yourself to a basket packed with cucumber sandwiches, good cheese, fresh berries and a split of champagne.

On a grey Sunday morning we photographed editors and artists reading and enjoying brunch in a nearly deserted skyscraper public garden. The easy menu was packed the night before: banana nut bread, bagels, orange juice, apricot jam blended with cream cheese, flaked salmon and cream cheese, and hot coffee. Ten minutes into the picnic it began to rain. Everyone grabbed the food and ran for cover in a nearby arcade and the picnic continued. Such urban centers usually are abandoned on weekends and offer visually interesting spaces for adventurous picnicking.

Workday Picnics

Millions of people are daily brown-baggers. Realistically speaking, every meal eaten from the ubiquitous bag or lunchbox is a picnic, whether it takes place at the desk, on an outdoor bench, in the employees' lunchroom or high on a steel girder. But there's no excuse for the same boring foods over and over — a little care can transform brown bag or lunchbox meals.

Although it gave its name to this type of noontime eating, the brown bag is really inferior to the lunchbox when it comes to carrying meals. Equipped with a collection of small, easy sealing containers for all kinds of foods, plastic or metal lunchboxes eliminate using paper, plastic wrap or other nonbiodegradable products. Additionally, the food stays fresher, does not leak out and chances of accidents are fewer. If you still like to carry a brown bag (lunchboxes are bulky), buy bags of recycled paper.

A stainless steel or sturdy plastic fork, knife and spoon, a real glass and a cloth napkin do much to upgrade the amenities of the usually hurried lunch.

Check out our ideas for lunchbox meals and let them improve the quality and interest of foods you take along or send out Monday through Friday. Also, refer to Sandwiching, pages 38 and 39.

An occasional in-house picnic for the office staff or other work group can boost morale and make long business hours pass faster. The office picnic can be a catered affair, a collection of treats selected from a good deli, or best yet, everyone's homemade specialties to share. Set up your workday banquet right in the office, on a conference table or even the floor. If it's a gorgeous day, however, and everyone can spare the time, let the answering service take over and head outdoors to a closeby sunny spot.

A birthday brunch in an eighteenth floor office was a real picnic in the sense of a portable feast. Friends brought Danish pastries, croissants, butter, jam, fresh fruit salad to go with the hot coffee. But the cake, crafted from candle-topped bagels generously with cream cheese, made it a birthday picnic.

Lunchbox Suggestions

☐ Hot food in preheated, individual-size, wide-mouth thermos: soups, consommés, chowder, spicy chili, beef stew, baked beans, spaghetti, macaroni and cheese, and other casserole-type dishes.

☐ Hot beverage in thermos: special coffee such as cappuccino or Irish coffee, spiced or plain tea, hot chocolate with cinnamon, mulled cider, wine or bouillon.

☐ Chilled food in precooled wide-mouth thermos: cold soups, meat or fish salads.

☐ Chilled beverage in thermos: lemonade, minted iced tea, freshly squeezed fruit or vegetable juices, cocktails, tropical punches, plain or chocolate milk.

☐ Bottled chilled beverages: sodas, juices, sparkling mineral water, splits of wine or champagne, sparkling apple juice.

☐ Salads: Three-bean, fresh fruit, potato, macaroni, rice, green pea, lentil. Green salads suggested only if you carry dressing in separate container for last minute tossing.

☐ Stuffed eggs: easier to carry when halved, filled and reassembled.

☐ Breads: homemade loaves in slices, muffins, corn-bread sticks, tortillas, Arab pocket bread, English crackers, biscuits, yeast rolls, brioche, croissants, bagels spread with cream cheese. And butter or margarine, of course.

☐ Homemade or plain yogurt (or sour cream) mixed with fresh berries or fruit instead of overly sweet dairy case variety.

☐ Ethnic foods, homemade or from international markets or restaurants: Japanese **sushi**, Italian **frittata**, Mexican **guacamole**, Russian eggplant caviar appetizer, to name a few.

☐ Cheeses: cubes, slices or wedges individually wrapped; cheese spreads in sealed containers.

☐ Tiny dispensers: salt and pepper, along with sugar or honey, if required.

☐ Individual tins: caviar, pâté, sardines or meat spreads.

☐ Finger foods: celery, zucchini, carrot and cucumber sticks, sliced kohlrabi, turnips or **jicama**, sweet or hot pepper strips or pods, asparagus spears, chilled steamed broccoli.

☐ Condiments: cucumber pickles of all types, marinated mushrooms or artichoke hearts, pickled peaches or pears, chutney, tomato **salsa** or relish, crunchy pickled okra pods, green pimento-stuffed olives, ripe olives stuffed with creamy herbed cheese.

☐ Desserts: fruits and cheeses, fruit compotes with liqueur, cupcakes, fruit and nut breads with cream cheese, cookies that don't crumble, chocolate truffles, plain cakes — angel food, fruit, pound, sponge.

Left: During the lunch hour downtown areas are filled every workday with brown baggers seeking a place in the sun. Serious weekday lunch carriers can collect a variety of handy food containers that simplify and add variety to noontime picnicking. A little planning and care can transform the daily lunch into an exciting movable feast.

Below: Consider this simple but elegant brown bag picnic. The menu consists of a bit of pâté on crackers, a carrot salad in a convenient plastic box, sparkling mineral water, a couple of fancy cookies and fresh strawberries. A cloth napkin, plate and glass, and plastic handled stainless utensils add the proper amenities.

Birthday at the Zoo

What seems more natural than combining a child's birthday with a visit to a zoo? The picnic area is built-in and there is plenty happening to keep everyone entertained. Most zoos offer areas for birthday groups but request that you phone ahead to reserve a place and time.

In planning children's picnics there are two basic rules: keep it simple, make it colorful. Coordinated paper tablecloths, plates and napkins, along with plastic flatware and glasses in bright, primary colors make decorating easy fun. Helium-filled balloons (from party shops) always give a lift to the festivities.

Plan a menu with true appeal. Hot dogs and kids just go together. (If you fill a thermos with boiling water and drop wieners into it before leaving home, they'll be piping hot and plump for serving once you reach the zoo.) Dill pickles on stakes (small dowels or heavyduty cooking chopsticks) make unusual lollipops, and potato chips, soft drinks or milk fill out the picnic.

Then comes the birthday cake (bakery supplied) with marzipan candy animals marching around the edge — guaranteed to delight.

Above: Squeals of delight ring through the children's zoo picnic grounds as birthday revelers chase elusive bubbles. Coordinated paper party ware in primary colored stripes and helium-filled balloons make decorating easy.
Right: Animals at the petting zoo often go to several birthday parties a day, but pickle lollipops may have been a new sight.
Left: Finally, it's time for the birthday cake! This one is chocolate with white icing topped with candy zoo animals.

Sweet Tooth Picnic

On Valentine's Day we invited a group of dedicated sweets lovers and staged a picnic of just desserts and coffee. The specialties of several bakeries were purchased and included chocolate mousse hearts, lemon cake, banana walnut cake, chocolate orange torte, fresh strawberries dipped in white chocolate, cheesecake, chocolate truffles and marzipan frogs.

Anyone with a real sweet tooth is sure to judge this the Perfect Picnic, outdoors or in. It could be a special midsummer birthday, Mother's Day, Valentine's Day, graduation or anytime you want to make a special day out of an ordinary one.

What could be easier? Simply set out a glorious array of sweets and plenty of hot coffee. There are several ways to go about this: select the specialties of nearby bakeries and pastry shops; or ask each guest to prepare and share favorite desserts, along with copies of recipes for exchanging; or show off your own baking skills with an assortment of homemade creations.

At home prepare hot coffee or a variety of special coffee drinks (café au lait, cappucino, Viennese coffee) and pour into heated thermoses. Be sure to carry along a supply of ice water, too. Sweets have a way of making you really thirsty.

Paper picnic supplies are obviously a lot easier, but your afternoon may merit the extra effort of real linens and dishes.

Midnight Picnic for New Year's Eve

When you'd prefer to spend the last few hours of the old year at home with very special friends far from the madding crowds, consider a picnic with great style and elegance. Spread it on a protected patio or terrace, arrange it with verve on the living room floor, set up a folding table in a warm greenhouse or, in mild southern climates, under the stars.

Perhaps, like us, you'll find that it's fun to follow a formal theme with everything in black and white. Request guests to dress in black and white — formal or costumed in fantasy as they like.

Pull out all the stops and present a cold seafood buffet on sparkling silver and crystal under a massive cloud of black and white balloons. Bring out all your best — silver serving pieces and flatware, china and crystal. For accent, add black lacquerware and white or black plastic bowls or vases. All the food can be prepared the day before and kept refrigerated until serving time to allow you to relax at your own party.

New Year's Eve Picnic for 8
Oysters on the Halfshell

Lobster Mousse

Caviar Stuffed Eggs / Ripe Olives
Chilled White Vegetables with Crab Mayonnaise

Scallop Seviche*

Crisp Crackers

Poached Pears

Champagne

(Recipe follows)

*See the Ortho book
Adventures in Mexican Cooking.

The bright red shell decorating the lobster mousse platter is the one note of color in this New Year's Eve black and white fantasy, the ultimate in luxurious picnicking. Lin Cotton is ready to greet his guests at the midnight picnic staged on a sheltered terrace. In keeping with the formal theme, large display penguins bedeck the table and a plastic top hat ice bucket holds the flowers.

Lobster Mousse

- 2 tablespoons unflavored gelatin
- ½ cup cold water
- 1½ cups mayonnaise
- ⅓ cup freshly squeezed lemon juice
- 1½ cup minced celery
- ½ minced onion
- 2½ to 3 cups cooked lobster meat (fresh, frozen or canned)
- ⅔ cup whipping cream, stiffly whipped
- Salt, pepper and paprika to taste
- Ripe olives (garnish)
- Lobster shell for decoration (if available)

1. Soak gelatin in cold water to soften, then dissolve in small pan over simmering water. Stir gelatin into the mayonnaise in large mixing bowl, blend in lemon juice and set aside.

2. Blend celery and onion with the minced lobster meat in a food processor with steel knife until smooth, or mince together very finely with a sharp knife. Add to the mayonnaise mixture. Fold in whipped cream and add salt, pepper and paprika to taste. Pour mousse into rinsed 2-quart mold and chill well.

3. To serve, unmold the mousse on a tray and decorate with a lobster shell, if one is available. Garnish the mousse with whole ripe olives.

Serves 12.

Poached Pears

Select well-formed, slightly underripe winter pears. Fruit that is ripened to the eating stage will fall apart when poached.

- 8 pears, peeled, stems intact
- Cold water and lemon juice
- 4 cups water
- 1 cup champagne or white wine
- 2½ cups sugar
- 4 teaspoons freshly squeezed lemon juice
- 1 teaspoon finely grated lemon rind
- 4 whole cloves
- 1 cinnamon stick

1. As soon as peeled, place pears in cold water containing a squeeze of lemon juice to prevent darkening.

2. In large saucepan combine 4 cups water, champagne or wine, sugar, lemon juice and rind; bring to boiling. Add spices, then the pears. Cover and cook at a gently rolling boil until pears are tender. Do not overcrowd fruit in the pan. (Boiling keeps the pears moving for even cooking. Cook pears in 2 batches if necessary.)

Poach until pears are tender and slightly translucent.

3. Remove pears carefully with a slotted spoon. Stand them up in a flat, shallow serving bowl or plate. (When cool, trim bottoms, if necessary, to help them stand up straight.) When all pears are cooked, pour a little of the poaching syrup over them and chill.

Serves 8.

Note: If you prefer, pears can be halved and cored before poaching. If desired, add a dollop of whipped cream or soft custard at serving time.

Alternative Menu Suggestions

■ Though sumptuous, this menu was planned to be light and fairly low-calorie in contrast to heavy holiday feasting. However, most of our guests agreed that we could have added a rich dessert. You may wish to include a favorite cake decorated in black or white, or at least some crunchy chocolate cookies to serve with the pears. If you're up to it, a chocolate soufflé hot from the oven would be grand just after midnight.

■ Instead of the lobster mousse, you may choose to offer a tray of cold cracked crab or whole lobster and let the guests do the work. Serve with lemon juice and creamy horseradish.

Vegetables with Crab Mayonnaise

Quickly rinse, dry and chill whatever fresh, white raw vegetables are available — Belgian endive, cauliflower florets, blanched asparagus — and add sliced canned hearts of palm. Arrange on a tray around a bowl of cold Crab Mayonnaise.

Crab Mayonnaise: To 1 cup of homemade or good quality prepared mayonnaise, add about 6 ounces of cooked, flaked crab meat (fresh or canned). Combine well with a little freshly squeezed lemon juice and cayenne pepper to taste.

Makes about 1½ cups.

Picnics on the Move

We are becoming a more active people all the time. With so much time devoted to jogging, tennis, skating, biking, horseback riding and other such self-improvement, it's often difficult to find time to eat. The obvious solution is to combine outdoor activity with good food. **Voila!** — a picnic!

Before starting out, take time to pack a meal. Stash it in the car, bicycle basket, saddlebag or tote. It can be as simple as a good sandwich, but it certainly doesn't have to stop there. For a special lift, fold up a cloth napkin, tuck in a split of champagne, or a container of something wonderfully rich. First the jogging or tennis — then the pleasant reward.

Of course, many active people are seriously dieting. Then the stage is set for a picnic of crunchy seasonal vegetables, juicy fruits, tender poached chicken and icy mineral water with a squeeze of lime, or other common sense, good-tasting fare. Just being outdoors helps you forget you're dieting.

Activity oriented picnics can be kept just for you, for two, or expanded into a party. Meet your friends on bicycles some gorgeous day and plan several stops along the way for an entire day of light picnicking. Carry along breakfast or a mid-morning snack in saddlebags or bike baskets. Stop at a deli for a tasty takeout lunch (ignore the heavy foods); then a few cookies in the afternoon; finally, a stop at one of the cyclist's homes for a backyard buffet that's been waiting in the refrigerator.

On a morning of horseback riding, tie up along the trail for a snack you've carried with you, or get together with friends back at the stables for a more sumptuous lunch that's been waiting in a basket in the car.

Traveling on planes, trains, and buses is a time to take advantage of your own well-packed meal instead of submitting to the usual dull fare. European train travelers have done this for years, pulling from hampers marvelous tempting tidbits often shared with wistful fellow tourists.

And who doesn't enjoy a picnic stop when traveling by car? Cold salads, pâté or ethnic specialties from delicatessens and markets, good cheese, crusty rolls, cold meats, fresh fruits, or even elaborate dishes can be packed for those on the go. Check out our sandwich ideas on page 38, and the brown bag suggestions on page 69. Many can be adapted to meals on wheels — or wings.

The roller skating craze is upon us, with the gaudy socks and knee pads that go with it. But even skaters take time out for hamburgers, chips, fresh fruit and high-energy yogurt shakes spread out on a rainbow striped beach towel. Paper plates and cups are easy to carry in a string tote bag.

With lightweight snacks from your well-stocked pantry stuff a pack for a quick get-away picnic along the bike path. You'll always be ready for impromptu picnicking if you keep a knife, can and bottle openers, napkins and other necessary items in your pack.

Tailgating with Style

With countless Americans flocking to sports events from coast to coast, the tailgate picnic has become a national pastime. Stadium parking lots are liberally dotted with festive groups spreading out food and spirits at the rear of station wagons, family autos, sports cars, campers and trucks.

With a little planning and attention to details of menu and table service, a tailgate picnic can be turned into something special. Haul out the good tableware, if you wish, or choose attractive paper goods. Pack a folding table and chairs for maximum comfort. Prepare old standards or try new recipes that taste good and look terrific. Tailgate picnicking with friends is a signal for pot luck, making it easy for everyone.

Likewise, family picnics can be planned around children's sports activities. Sometimes it's the only way an active family can all be together for a meal! Throw down a cloth or blanket on the sidelines, well out of the playing area. Plan on plenty of food to calm ravenous appetites at game's end.

Right: Parking lots of sports coliseums around the country are dotted generously with tailgate picnics before every game. This car trunk is loaded with all-American picnic fare—hamburgers to cook on the portable barbecue, macaroni salad, chips and beer.

Above: About as stylish as tailgating can get are the lavish spreads that accompany the *Concours d'Elegance* at the Pebble Beach polo grounds in California. Vintage cars and good eating seem to go hand in hand. These picnickers have packed a banquet for a group of friends into three baskets. The velvet throw, silver goblets and fresh flowers transform a patch of lawn into an elegant outdoor dining room.

Above: Meals at sporting events come in all sizes and styles. Parents can pack a supper to share with friends along the sidelines, leaving plenty of food for famished players after the game.

Right: At Cornell University in Ithaca, New York, we photographed a portable feast in the parking lot. Card tables held an array of picnic foods, both hot and cold. Game fans don't usually bring along the fine silver, but this was a special day—Homecoming.

Waterbound Picnics

There's something not only tranquil, but truly magical about dining near water. Clambakes and other oceanside feasts are all-time favorites, as are picnics by inland streams, lakes and ponds. But a picnic **in** the water takes on another dimension.

Good food somehow seems more sensual and special when you're isolated in a canoe on a lake, on a boat at sea, or even partially immersed in a backyard pool or hot tub.

The West Coast hot tub phenomenon is moving cross-country with rapid speed. Owners soon discover the pleasures of dining in the relaxing waters. Children especially love eating in the big tub. Why not float a birthday cake on a life-preserver? Or plan a fancy dessert for adults served from a deckside buffet or on a floating innertube table — an incomparable picnic beneath a canopy of twinkling stars.

An inflatable raft can serve as a party buffet table in a swimming pool on a hot afternoon. There are also commercially made tables with indents to hold glasses and rails to keep plates in place. Treat your guests to cool tropical drinks and light appetizers in the pool, the rest of the picnic served poolside.

Right: The boat definitely is not seaworthy, but it makes a convenient floating buffet. Louis hauls it to a shady spot on a nearby gravelly island for a hot day lunch in late summer.

Above: In a colander the fruit, bottled and canned beverages are lowered into the shallow stream to cool. Lunch also includes bread sticks wrapped in thinly sliced ham, bean salad, sliced tomatoes, almond crescent cookies and melon.

Above: With fishing gear and picnic hamper in hand and Farfie on leash, the Pillon family heads to a boat for a Saturday on the water. Judy plans and prepares the picnic ahead so she has time to read while Roger and the boys, Jay and Mike, fish. The microwave oven on board is a help for fast-heating food on a cold day.

Right: Tai, Min and Keelja enjoy an after-school picnic while splashing in the hot tub. Giant chocolate chip cookies always score a big hit, and icy lemonade is especially refreshing when you are in warm, steamy water.

Wine Tasting Tour

Vineyards from California to New York, from the Pacific Northwest to Michigan and Ohio, fascinate both locals and tourists any time of the year, but especially at harvest when the vines are laden with grapes and the leaves are beginning their vivid display. Visitors can spend several hours exploring wineries that are open to the public, discovering an occasional bottle to buy, and then stopping for a personal, leisurely taste-testing picnic.

Before leaving home, pack a basket with the essentials: a cloth, some napkins, wine glasses, a knife, a corkscrew. Wine goes with cheese like a hand in a glove, and most vineyard areas have a full quota of cheese shops. Stop en route for a good assortment,

both old favorites and something new, crusty bread, crisp crackers and fresh fruits. For inventive combinations, see the cheese and wine charts on pages 90 to 92.

Many wineries have designated picnic areas and some will even provide food to purchase. Be sure to get permission to use a site before unloading your picnic.

If you don't live in wine country you can still enjoy all the pleasures of a wine-tasting outing. Visit a wine merchant and let him suggest several bottles each of red and white wines. Call some friends, pack up the basket and head for your favorite local picnic spot to sip and consider the comparative merits of your choices.

Opposite: Heartland of the California wine country, the Napa Valley offers marvelous picnic sites. Many scenic places, such as the historic Bale Mill, provide picnic tables for visitors on wine-tasting excursions.
Right: At harvest time, the heady aroma of fresh grapes intensifies the flavor of wine and cheese. Mary and Michael Landis (left) carried a low table into the vineyard for a late afternoon snack with son Josh and friends Cynthia Borcich and Angela.

Picnicking Along the Trail

A day of hiking, climbing or just plain prowling through the woods works wonders with an appetite. You'll want to load a small knapsack or day pack with nutritional quick-energy foods that are lightweight and easy to carry. No hiker wants to be weighed down with bulky, heavy containers.

Handy hiking equipment and camping gadgets make food transportation a snap. Check hardware stores, camp suppliers, surplus stores, or ski shops for convenient, lightweight collapsible cups and stacked, compact plates that double for eating and storing food. The versatile Swiss army knife is almost indispensable; there is an attachment for every need (plus a plastic-ivory toothpick!). Look for plastic tubes that can be filled and sealed from the bottom to hold honey, peanut butter, jam or jelly, thin pâtés, cheese, mustard. Just squeeze onto crackers, bread or fruit.

Plastic canteens, flasks and small thermoses solve the drinking problem. They're nearly weightless and a hiker can carry his own liquid supply. For a little extra dash, tuck in a tea towel to spread on a flat rock or tree stump and thin cotton bandanas for napkins. They add a touch of class and reduce trash takeout.

Health or natural food stores as well as supermarkets are good places to find ready-to-go energy foods. Self-sealing or tied plastic bags are the best containers for trail foods (also sandwiches, cut vegetables and fruit). Anything foil wrapped should be labeled. Small plastic containers with sealing lids are good for trail foods, too, but they add bulk.

Recommended Knapsack Foods

Raw vegetables cut into small pieces

Roasted soybeans, fried peas, any unsalted nuts

Cereals, toasted and seasoned, to eat out of hand

High-energy trail mix

Quick-energy candy bars and cookies

Dry salami and cubes of dry Monterey jack cheese

Flat bread — Mexican flour tortillas and Arab pocket bread

Dried fruit snack

Apricots, banana chips, apples, pears, dates, raisins, pineapple, ginger

Jerky and smoked meats

Hot beverages — tea (black, green, or herbal), cider, chocolate, coffee, bouillon

Cold beverages — cider, fruit juice, punch, wine, mineral water, powdered drink mixes

(Recipe follows)

Food to Avoid

Anything that requires refrigeration

Bulky foods

Soft-skinned or overripe fruits

Overly moist sandwiches

Cakes or pies with cream

Salty chips that crumble or cause thirst

Could there be a more inspiring rest stop for midday eating, reading and relaxing than the base of a towering giant redwood?

Dried Fruit Snack

In a large bowl combine ½ cup each dark and golden raisins, chopped dried apricots and pears, 1 cup each dried banana chips, shredded coconut and chopped pitted dates. Store in airtight container.

Makes about 5 cups.

High-Energy Trail Mix

Create your own special mix by combining equal portions of several of the following: raisins, almonds, chocolate or carob chips, sunflower seeds, pecans, walnuts.

This energizing snack can be made in quantity, stored in airtight containers and kept fresh-tasting for 2 weeks or more (if you can keep your hands out of the jar). Package into small plastic bags and tuck into the knapsack's outer pockets.

Hikers' Granola

Add any other nuts, dried fruit, seeds or cereals you wish to this basic recipe.

2 cups rolled oats
1 cup each **honey, shredded coconut, sunflower seeds and wheat germ**
½ cup each **raisins, sesame seeds, slivered almonds and salad oil**

Combine all ingredients in a mixing bowl and stir to thoroughly blend. Spread in a shallow pan and bake at 325°F/165°C for about 20 minutes, stirring often. Cool and store in airtight container.

Makes about 8 cups.

After a day on a long, hot Sierra Nevada trail these mountain climbers deserved a filling, leisurely meal at sunset.

Above: Somewhere along the trail, hikers Margaret and Alan spread out their high-energy picnic on a log. Foods were packaged in self-sealing plastic bags, wrapped in the terrycloth dishtowel that doubled as a picnic cloth, and tucked into the day-packs.
Left: A waist-high stump near a lake makes a perfect dining table after an afternoon of fishing.

Meat Jerky

Prepare with beef or venison.

1. Slice 3 pounds of meat (flanks, brisket or round steak) with the grain into ⅛ to ¼-inch strips. Remove all fat.

2. Marinate overnight in a mixture of 1 table-spoon salt, 3 cloves garlic, pressed, ¼ cup soy sauce, black pepper to taste and enough water to cover meat. Turn slices several times.

3. Drain well and place uncrowded on a wire rack on a foil-lined bak-ing sheet. Bake at oven's lowest temperature for 12 hours, opening the door occasionally to cool and allow moisture to escape. Cool jerky and store in airtight container in refrigerator; keeps indefinitely.

For other suitable trail food recipes, see Ortho's **12 Month's Harvest** and **Adventures in Oriental Cooking.**

What If It Rains?

No matter how often you sing for it not to rain on your picnic, you know sooner or later it's bound to happen, with varying complications. Caught in a sudden shower in a city park merely means a retreat to the nearest shelter. But when you're in the wilds, a storm can make a picnic's life span short and unhappy — find a tree or bushes before the sandwiches get too soggy, or quickly rescue the food and retreat to the car.

When you wake up some morning and feel a picnic coming on, only to discover that it's raining, don't despair. If it's damp and only a bit drizzly, go prepared with painters' plastic dropcloths, a surplus parachute or canvas tarpaulins in the car trunk. Tie them between trees or attach to poles to form a canopy.

The easiest solution, obviously, is to stay home. Find a cozy spot where you can enjoy the downpour. The living room floor will do. Consider picnicking by a crackling fireplace, on a blanket with all the usual picnic gear helping create the proper mood.

Opposite: Undaunted by a long spell of rainy weather these determined picnickers simply spread a cheerful cloth on the sunroom floor. From the kitchen came a basket with the lunch. George the parrot, as well as the creative picnickers, had a great time in spite of the rain.

Above: Every home has someplace to spread a rainy day repast. An enclosed courtyard provided protection from the rain when a downpour halted Martha's plan for a drive in the country. Left: The weather outside was cold and wet, but the fire was so delightful that a picnic seemed in order for Jim and Karen. *Broodjes*, thin ham slices on butter-rich soft rolls, potato salad, apples and Danish cookies were served from a wicker tray.

Picnicker's Guide to Shopping and Planning

About the time this book got underway, as if some form of ESP were at work, the daily "Question Man" column of The San Francisco Chronicle asked passersby, "Could you write a book?" The first answer in the column came from a grandmother visiting from Pittsburg, California.

"I could write a book about bad picnics. I've been on lots of them. You stay up half the night cooking and getting ready, don't get half enough sleep and there's never any place to go to the bathroom and it's always hot and there's never a place to sit down and your back kills you and radio's turned up loud and kids yelling and the father tries to play ball with the kids and throws his back out."

While we can't do anything to control the antics of fathers, we do hope to provide help for some of the other problems. A successful picnic depends not only on good food, good company and the proper setting, but on planning, too. Attention to nitty gritty details can make all the difference between a disaster and an enjoyable day. It's too bad the Pittsburg grandmother didn't have the chance to read the following tips on organizing, the checklists for food and the guide to purchasing equipment.

Above: Whether you're packing, shopping for food or planning other details of outdoor dining, this chapter is designed to offer time and energy saving tips to make your picnicking easier and more fun.
Opposite: While this book was being produced, writer James McNair packed innumerable picnic baskets. This proved to be one of his favorites because it is sturdy and holds a lot.

Shopping is Half the Fun

Picnics imply pleasure, so it follows that shopping can be as much fun as the event itself. You get the chance to explore marvelous delicatessens and food markets, savoring all their heady flavors and odors. Taste-testing cheeses and cold meats is really an instant mini-picnic for the shopper.

There's something, also, that most of us love about roaming through hardware and surplus stores. Finding just the right equipment or gadget is a pre-outing pleasure. Your shopping adventure also could take you through fancy gift shops, sporting goods stores, flea markets, paper product party shops, department stores, fabric and linen shops, and most fascinating of all, gourmet kitchen stores filled with items destined to upgrade your present picnic style.

If you're not a passionate shopper, you don't even have to take off your slippers and leave your fireside. Mail-order catalogs show canned, smoked, dried, frozen and fresh food specialties that make great picnic fare. (See sources, page 93.) In addition, use the telephone book yellow pages to check out stores in your area that handle distinctive foods and supplies.

Right now, come along on a sit-down shopping spree.

Ready-to-go Food and Drinks

There are times when you don't feel like cooking or you're pushed for time, or you simply have a last-minute urge to get away and picnic. Sometimes you've prepared several dishes and need one or two more, something special to supplement your picnic. Although there may be times when the ever present fast-food chain is in order, there are many excellent alternatives.

Get to Know a Deli

The delicatessen, self-contained or part of a grocery or restaurant, is a traditional source of ready-to-serve foods for al fresco dining. You can stage an impromptu picnic by stopping en route; or plan an elaborate deli-based feast and make your selections the day before.

Prepared deli food is sold both by weight and liquid measure, packaged in containers or wrapped individually. Tell the clerk how many people you plan to feed and he will pack the proper amounts. When buying in quantity, you often can carry in your own sealable plastic containers or jars to be filled. (See also "Food for a Crowd," page 102.)

Quality varies greatly from deli to deli and you're a lucky picnic planner if you know a good one nearby. Smart shopping requires insistence on freshness, especially with mixed meat and vegetable salads, condiments and other highly perishable items. At many delis you can taste-test before buying, especially if you're a frequent customer.

Caution: Keep all perishable foods on ice if you plan to delay eating for more than an hour. (See page 104.)

Look for bargains on breads, cheeses, cold meats and other items to be frozen for later use. Buy in quantity and package in appropriate sizes for future outings. This allows you to defrost only what is needed — one picnic at a time.

A Deli Sampler

Here is a sample survey of what is found in a typical city delicatessen. Offerings vary according to available foods and eating habits of the region, size of the community, ethnic background of the owner or cook and demands of the patrons. For menu planning, choose compatible items from each column or mix and match to fill your hamper. (See also "Instant Picnics" chart on page 89.)

A good neighborhood delicatessen is a big bonus for the picnic planner. Get to know what's offered by all the sources at your disposal to supplement home cooking or furnish the complete meal.

Cold Meats (In made-to-order sandwiches, takeout tray arrangements or sliced and wrapped; usually sold sliced to your order by weight beginning at ¼ pound. Wrapped in plastic or butcher wrap.)

Deli-cooked meats are expensive in comparison to home-prepared but offer buyers variety and convenience.

Bologna	**Pastrami**
Canadian-style bacon	**Prosciutto**
Chicken, roasted	**Roast beef**
Corned beef	**Salami**
Ham, smoked, boiled or baked	**Sausages**
Liverwurst	**Turkey, roasted or smoked**
Mortadella	
Olive loaf, other luncheon meats	

Meat and Fish Salads (Good alone or as sandwich fillings; **must be fresh**. Sold by weight.)

Chicken	**Herring**	**Shrimp**
Crab	**Lobster**	**Tuna**
Ham	**Salmon**	**Turkey**

Fruit and Vegetable Salads (Sold in containers beginning at ¼-pound size.)

Aspic with meat or vegetables	**Hearts of palm**
Carrot and raisin	**Macaroni**
Cole slaw	**Mixed greens**
Cucumber	**Potato**
Egg	**Rice**
Fresh Fruit	**Tomato**
German potato	**Three-bean**
Green bean	**Vegetables, fruit in gelatin**
Green pea	

Pickles and Condiments (Sold in containers by size or weight.)

Eggplant caviar (also called eggplant dip and caponata)	**Olives: green and ripe, whole and pitted, stuffed, Greek, Sicilian**
Kosher dill pickles	**Pickled beets**
Marinated mushrooms, cauliflower, artichoke hearts and bottoms, herring, mixed vegetables, beans	**Roasted Italian peppers**
	Sauerkraut
	Sweet bread and butter pickles
Mustard pickles	

Cheeses (Sold by weight in containers, pre-wrapped packages or cut-to-order wedges, slabs or slices. See cheese chart, pages 90-91.)

Bola	Gorgonzola
Boursault	Gouda
Boursin	Gourmandise
Camembert	Gruyère
Cheddar	Jarlsberg
Edam	Monterey Jack
Emmenthal	Provolone
Feta	Roquefort
Fontina	Tilsit

Plus dozens of other domestics and imports, as well as cottage and creamed cheeses, cheese balls and pasteurized spreads.

Breads (Also check local bakeries, as well as grocery shelves.)

Bagels	Nine-grain
Banana	Oatmeal
Biscuits	Onion
Black	Panettone (Italian sweet
Brioche	bread)
Buns for burgers, hot	Pita (Arab pocket bread)
dogs	Potato
Challah (Jewish braided	Pumpernickel
white loaf)	Raisin
Cheese	Rolls
Cornbread	Rye, dark, light
Croissants	Sourdough
Date-nut	Swedish limpa
French loaf, baguette,	White
rolls (sweet and sour)	Whole wheat
Herb	Yogurt
Honey-wheat	
Italian loaf, breadsticks	

Desserts (Most delicatessens do not carry a wide selection. Check also with bakeries and pastry shops. Often cakes and pies can be purchased in halves or slices.)

Baklava, other Near East	Danish pastries
pastries	English trifle
Brownies, other bar	French pastries
cookies	Fruit turnovers
Butter cookies	Giant cookies
Cakes	Glacéed fruits
Candies	Pies
Chocolate truffles	Puddings
Coffeecake	Scottish shortbread
Cupcakes	

Miscellaneous Main-Dish Items

Barbecued chicken	Pizza
Boiled shrimp	Quiche (cheese pie,
Cooked lobster tails	often with bacon
Cornish pasties	or ham)
Cracked crab	Ravioli
Eggs, hard-cooked,	Scotch eggs (hard-
in aspic, stuffed	cooked eggs wrapped
Enchiladas	in sausage and fried)
Gefilte fish	Smoked salmon, trout,
Italian frittata	whitefish, eel
(omelet)	Stuffed grape leaves
Kippered herring	Turnovers, vegetable,
Pâtés	beef, chicken

Some delicatessens will pack a complete picnic meal in your own basket or one that you purchase from them.

Instant Picnics from the Deli

As an example of picnicking made easy, here are a half dozen items in various categories that are compatible no matter how you combine them. Choose one or more from each column and you'll be set for a ready-to-go outdoor meal.

Appetizer	Salad	Dessert
Cheese ball	Carrot and raisin	Chocolate chip cookies
Eggs in aspic	Cole slaw	Fruit turnovers
Marinated herring	Fresh fruit	Rice pudding
Marinated mushrooms	Macaroni	Danish pastries
Pâté	Potato	Apples, other fruit
Smoked salmon	Three-bean	Cupcakes

Main Dish	Bread	Beverages
Baked ham	Croissants	Apple juice
Chicken salad	French loaf	Cold beer
Barbecued chicken	Onion rolls	Mineral water
Meat pies	Pita (Arab bread)	Sodas
Roast beef	Whole wheat	Hot coffee
Quiche	Sliced rye	Chilled white wine

A Word on Cheese

In addition to the usually limited selection of cheeses available in supermarkets and most delicatessens, many shops are now exclusively devoted to cheese and there are special sections in larger department stores. Wherever you choose to buy cheese, here are two important points to remember.

First, find a reliable cheese merchant. Unless you know a lot about the subject, it's wise to get advice about what complements which food. To assure you of cheeses still in their prime, the store should have an active turnover of stock.

Second, sample cheese, if at all possible, before you buy. This usually presents no problem in good cheese stores or cheese departments. Wrapped cheeses will have to be judged by appearance, touch and smell.

Naturally aged or nonprocessed cheeses need proper storing to preserve freshness. Wrap tightly in foil or plastic to force out all air. Place wrapped pieces in a plastic bag or container and seal tightly. (Or store in an old-fashioned cheese keeper with a place in the bottom for fresh water.) Keep bags or containers of cheese on bottom shelf of refrigerator. Bring to room temperature before serving — simply take the cheese out of the refrigerator when packing up. Wrap any remaining cheese immediately after the picnic and place in the ice chest or return it to the refrigerator as soon as possible.

Most cheese freezes quite well. Cut into serving-size pieces and wrap tightly. To thaw, transfer from the freezer to the refrigerator 24 to 48 hours before the picnic.

A Guide to Picnic Cheeses

Type and Name	Origin	Characteristics	Suggested Beverages
Soft-Ripened			
Camembert	France	Mild to pungent, distinctive flavors; creamy interior; thin, white crust (edible if not too dry)	Light, fruity red wines; sparkling wines; dessert wines
Pont l'Evêque	France		
Livarot	France		
Brie	France		
Coulommiers	France		
Carré de l'Est	France		
Caprice des Dieux	France		
Vacherin	France, Switzerland		
Assertive			
Liederkranz	U.S.	Robust, highly aromatic flavor; soft, smooth, spreadable texture	Beer, ale
Limburger	Belgium		
Schloss	U.S. (Calif.)		
Triple-Crème			
Rondelé	U.S.	Flavored with garlic and herbs or pepper; soft, creamy, spreadable texture	Light red wines; dry white wines
Alouette	U.S.		
Boursin	France		
Boursault	France		
Bellétoile	France		
Spiced or Flavored			
Nokkelost	Norway	Flavored with caraway seeds	Beer or dry white wines
Leiden	Netherlands	With caraway, cloves, anise and/or cumin seeds	
Beau Pasteur	France	Various fruit and nut flavors added (cherry, orange, walnut) to rich processed cheese base	Dry white or sparkling wines
Gourmandise	France		
La Grappe	France	Coated with grape seeds	

Opposite: Stock up when you find a special sale on good cheese. Wrap it well and store in the refrigerator or cut into small pieces, wrap and freeze.

An assortment of cheeses, bread or crackers, fruit and a glass of wine make a near-perfect picnic.

Semi-Soft

Münster/Muenster	France/U.S. (Wisc.)	Mild to mellow, nutlike flavors; smooth, waxy texture; creamy to pale yellow color	Dry white wines; light, fruity red wines; light beer
Brick	U.S. (Wisc.)		
Monterey Jack	U.S. (Calif.)		
Oka	Canada		
Saint Paulin	France		
Reblochon	France		
Port Salut	France		
Esrom	Denmark		
Havarti	Denmark		
Tilsit	Germany		
Edam	Netherlands		
Gouda	Netherlands		
Bel Paese	Italy		
Taleggio	Italy		

Blue-Veined

Gorgonzola	Italy	White to creamy interior, marbled with blue-green mold; moist, semi-soft, crumbly texture; piquant flavor	Full-bodied red wines
Stilton	England		
Roquefort	France		
Blue	U.S.		

Swiss

Emmenthal	Switzerland	Firm texture with gas holes or "eyes" ranging in size from large to tiny (in Gruyère), slightly sweet, nutlike flavor	Chilled dry white and rosé wines
Jarlsberg	Norway		
Appenzeller	Switzerland		
Gruyère	Switzerland		
Fontina	Italy		

Cheddar

Cheddar	England, U.S.	Smooth, firm, sometimes crumbly in sharp aged versions; creamy white to orange color; mild to sharp flavor	Fruity red wines; hard or nonalcoholic cider
Colby	U.S. (Wisc.)		
Tillamook	U.S. (Ore.)		
Cheshire	England		
Caerphilly	Wales		

Goat and Sheep's Milk Cheeses

Feta	Greece	White, soft, salty, crumbly	Fruity red wines
Kasseri	Greece	Firm but crumbly; sharp flavor	
Valencay	France	Mild goat cheese, soft; gray ash-coated rind	
Banon	France	Small, mild goat or sheep's milk cheese; wrapped in chestnut leaves, tied with raffia	
Chabichou	France	Small, soft, cone-shaped goat cheese; strong fruity to sharp flavor	

Hard

Parmesan	Italy	Used mostly for grating, but supple enough to slice when young; white to creamy color; sharp, piquant flavor	Full-bodied red wines
Asiago	Italy		
Romano	Italy		

Picnic Beverages

Icy cold or piping hot drinks are important parts of any picnic. Keep a supply of drinks, instant mixes or almost-instant ingredients on hand.

If you enjoy wine, stock a picnicker's mini-cellar of favorites that are compatible with cheese and other picnic fare. (See chart, below.) A bottle or two of chilled white can be kept in the refrigerator, but not indefinitely. Or stop en route at a wine shop for chilled rosés, whites and sparkling wines. If your purchases weren't refrigerated, put them in the cooler so they'll be ready to serve when you reach the picnic site. Of course, red wine is always ready to pour.

The current mineral water craze in America is certainly nothing new to European picnickers. It's one of the most refreshing outdoor beverages, and contains no calories. Try several domestic and imported kinds; some are slightly salty, some more bubbly than others.

Cold sodas, fruit juices, even canned iced tea and cocktails are available in supermarkets and other stores along your picnic route. Keep a corkscrew, bottle and can openers in the car to cover emergencies.

Beverage Bottle Bag

1. Cut 1 rectangle and 1 circle from washable quilted fabric.
2. With right sides facing, seam ends of rectangle.
3. On inside, fold over 1-inch top hem and stitch.
4. Fit circle to inside bottom of bag, pin in place; stitch.
5. Turn bag to right side. On outside, split open small hole in side seam in hem. Insert a 15-inch long cord for a drawstring and handle. (For additional bottle protection, add a lining of foam rubber padding cut to fit inside.)

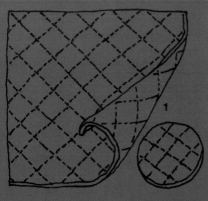

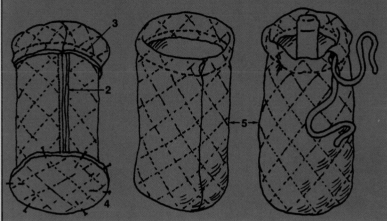

A Guide to U.S. Picnic Wines

Type or Variety	Characteristics	Suggested Foods
White (serve chilled)		
Chablis*	Light, clean, fruity, usually dry	Fish, shellfish, poultry, salads, cheese
Grey Riesling	Light, fresh, delicate, versatile	Poultry, white fish, salads
Johannisberg Riesling	Faintly sweet, piquant, fresh, fruity	Fish, poultry, shellfish
French Colombard	Perfumy, aromatic, off-dry	Well-seasoned poultry, shellfish
Chenin Blanc	Light, fruity; dry to fairly sweet, depending on vintner's style	Fresh fruit, poultry, shellfish
Pinot Blanc	Dry, reminiscent of Chardonnay	Fish, chicken, cheese
Sauvignon Blanc/ Fumé Blanc	Dry to fairly sweet (drier wines usually designated Fumé Blanc or Blanc Fumé)	Fish, shellfish, chicken
Chardonnay	Dry, elegant	Rich fish and shellfish dishes, poultry, cheese
Gewürztraminer	Spicy, dry to off-dry	Spicy foods, cold meats, spiced and semi-soft cheeses
Red (serve at room temperature)		
Burgundy*	Ranges from dry to slightly sweet; from light to full-bodied, depending on vintner's style	Red meats, cold meats, cheese
Gamay Beaujolais	Light, fresh, fruity	Cheese, cold meats, lamb
Zinfandel	Fairly dry, fresh, light to robust	Charcoal-grilled meats; stews
Cabernet Sauvignon	Dry, full-bodied, distinctive, elegant	Beef, lamb
Petite Sirah	Dry, usually full-bodied	Beef, game
Pinot Noir	Dry, soft, delicate	Steak, other red meats, cheese
Barbera	Full-bodied, dry, grapey	Italian dishes with tomato sauce
*Widely available in less expensive jug versions.		
Rosé (serve chilled)**		
Grenache Rosé	Relatively sweet, fragrant	Fruits, ham
Gamay Rosé	Fresh, slightly sweet	Cold dishes, salads with fruit, chicken, cheese
**Also rosés of Cabernet, Zinfandel, Pinot Noir, Gewürztraminer		
Sparkling		
Sparkling	Dryness ranges from SEC (sweetest) through EXTRA DRY to BRUT and NATURAL (driest)	Serve as apéritif, with hors d'oeuvres, fish or shellfish, poultry; with elegant desserts

(See also "Guide to Sherries," page 49.)

The well-stocked get-away pantry always contains an assortment of bottled, canned and packaged beverages.

Restaurant Prepared Picnics
If given ample notice, many restaurants will prepare their specialties for take-out. Choose dishes that don't need reheating and are best served cold, at room temperature or only slightly warm. Arrange to pick up the prepared foods on the way to the picnic. Restaurants often will pack food in your own containers and picnic hamper. (See our Spanish picnic, page 48.)

The International Marketplace
In addition to ethnic restaurants, markets and delis, you can often find good cooks of foreign descent who will prepare some of their national dishes for a grand picnic. Or perhaps you would like to take a class in French, Italian or Chinese cookery, frequently offered at community colleges, adult night schools and private cooking classes. In addition, see the mail-order sources.

Shopping for Food by Mail
Foods via mail order can bring hard-to-locate ingredients to your door. Offerings include international seasonings and ingredients — French pâtés and truffles, Iranian caviar, unusual Chinese sauces. Some regional mail-order houses offer American specialties that make marvelous picnic eating: New England shellfish, Wisconsin cheeses, Smithfield Virginia ham, California avocados.

Check gourmet food magazines for current mail-order advertisers or write for catalogs from the following sources. (There may be a charge for some catalogs. All addresses were correct at time of publication.)

Mail-Order Foods

Ozark Mountain Smoke House Inc.
P.O. Box 37
Farmington, AR 72730
501/267-3339
[Smoked bacon, ham, sausage, turkey]

I. Magnin
Gourmet Foods
Union Square
San Francisco, CA 94128
415/362-2100
[Fauchon: candies, pâté, preserved fruits, other gourmet items]

Liberty House
Gourmet Department
120 Stockton Street
San Francisco, CA 94108
415/772-2245
[Fortnum & Mason Ltd: teas, preserves]

Narsai's Market
389 Colusa Avenue
Berkeley, CA 94707
415/527-3737
[Tea, coffee, chocolate, canned delicacies; variety of baskets]

Williams-Sonoma
Mail Order Department
P.O. 3732
San Francisco, CA 94119
415/982-0295
[Imported herbs and gourmet items]

Marshall Field & Co.
Gourmet Department
11 S. State Street
Chicago, IL 60621
312/781-1000
[Fauchon, Fortnum & Mason Ltd: teas, mustards]

Wilton Enterprises
833 West 115th Street
Chicago, IL 60643
[Cake decorating supplies]

Batistela's Sea Foods, Inc.
910 Touro Street
New Orleans, LA 70116
504/949-2724
[Crayfish and Louisiana seafood]

Kate Latter's Candy & Gift Store
300 Royal Street
New Orleans, LA 70130
504/525-5359
[Cakes, coffee, Creole condiments, preserves, pralines, soups]

Especially Maine
U.S. Route 1
Arundel, ME 04046
207/985-3749
[Blueberries, maple syrup, puddings, beans]

Saltwater Farm
Varrell Lane
York Harbor, ME 03911
207/363-3182
[Live lobster, smoked salmon, soups, shellfish]

Omaha Steaks International
4400 South 96th Street
Omaha, NE 68127
402/331-1010
[Beef, lamb, quail, smoked salmon, ham, bacon, smoked turkey]

Epicures' Club
939 Lehigh Avenue
Union, NJ 07083
201/686-3400
[Smoked pheasant, pâté, condiments, cheeses, puddings, other specialties]

B. Altman & Co.
Delicacies Department
361 Fifth Street
New York, NY 10016
212/679-7800
[Fortnum & Mason Ltd: teas, preserves, relishes, cakes]

Bloomingdales
Delicacies Department
59th Street & Lexington
New York, NY 10022
212/223-7111
[Fauchon: mustard, honey, jams]

Caviarteria
870 Madison Avenue
New York, NY 10021
212/861-1210
[Caviar, cheese, pâté]

Maison Glass
52 East 58th Street
New York, NY 10022
212/755-3316
[Caviar, cheese, condiments, cookies, herbs and spices, canned pâté, smoked game]

Paprikas Weiss
1546 Second Avenue
New York, NY 10028
212/288-6903
[Candies, caviar, dried fruits, herbs and spices, tinned meats, other delectables]

Plumbridge Confections & Gifts
33 East 61st Street
New York, NY 10021
212/371-0608
[Chocolate truffles]

Poriloff Caviar
542 LaGuardia Place
New York, NY 10012
212/254-7171
[Caviar]

The Harry and David Co.
2518 S. Pacific Highway
Medford, OR 97501
503/776-2121
[Cakes, candies, cheese, dried and fresh fruits, smoked fowls, nuts, pastries, preserves, puddings]

Weaver's Famous Lebanon Bologna
P.O. Box 525
Lebanon, PA 17042
717/272-5643
[Bacon, ham, dried beef, assorted meats]

The Vermont Country Store
Weston, VT 05161
802/824-6932
[Maple syrup, maple candy, cheese, mincemeat, whole grains]

Smithfield Ham & Products Co. Inc.
P.O. Box 487
Smithfield, VA 23430
804/357-2121
[Ham, bacon, relishes]

Hegg and Hegg Smoked Salmon
801 Marine Drive
Port Angeles, WA 98362
206/457-3344
[Smoked salmon, seafood]

Recreational Equipment, Inc.
1525 Eleventh Avenue
Seattle, WA 98122
206/323-8333
[Freeze dried and dehydrated meals suitable for backpack picnicking]

Figi's
630 S. Central Street
Marshfield, WI 54449
715/387-6311
[Cheese, smoked duck and turkey, dried and fresh fruits, ham, sausage, pastries, preserves]

The Swiss Colony
1112 Seventh Avenue
Monroe, WI 53566
608/328-8500
[Cakes, candies, cheese, cookies, honey, smoked meats, nuts, preserves]

Mail-Order Equipment and Supplies

Forrest Jones Inc.
3274 Sacramento Street
San Francisco, CA 94115
415/567-2483
[Picnic baskets, cooking and serving equipment; supplier of many items shown in this book]

Williams-Sonoma
Mail Order Department
P.O. 3732
San Francisco, CA 94119
415/982-0295
[Cooking and serving equipment]

Bridge Kitchen Ware Company
212 East 52nd Street
New York, NY 10022
212/688-4220
[Equipment for cooking and serving]

Paprikas Weiss Importer
1546 Second Avenue
New York, NY 10028
212/288-6903
[Gourmet cookware and utensils]

The Perfect Picnic Pantry

While it's always nice to have the luxury of planning and preparing well in advance, often the best outings are the "Hey, let's go on a picnic!" inspirations — a hurried raid on the refrigerator and cupboard, then off to some pleasant patch of grass and a shady tree.

Admittedly there's nothing better than a really good tuna sandwich, some pickles, a piece of fruit and an icy drink, but the occasional stocking of your larder can do a lot to add variety and improve the quality of your quick escapes. If you're prone to picnic improvisation, here are some good items to keep on hand.

A quick raid on the perfect picnic pantry should produce nearly everything that is needed for outdoor dining and to minimize preparation time.

In the Refrigerator:

Beverages (sodas, beer, mineral water)

Breads, muffins, rolls

Butter or margarine

Catsup, Worcestershire, soy sauce

Cheeses (wedges, slices, spreads; cream cheese for easy dips and spreads)

Cold meats (well wrapped), smoked meats, whole salami

Eggs (raw and hard-cooked)

Fruit

Lemons and limes

Milk and cream

Mustard, mayonnaise, other spreads

Pickles, olives, relishes

Salad makings, sandwich garnishes (lettuce, watercress, spinach, sprouts, fresh herbs, cucumbers, tomatoes)

Vegetables (carrots, celery, cauliflower, turnips, zucchini)

Wine (white and rosé)

In the Freezer:

Breads (homebaked or frozen dough)

Cakes, cookies, other desserts

Cheeses (wrapped in small portions, grated)

Chopped onions, peppers, minced herbs

Coffee, beans or ground

Crêpes

Homemade broths and soups

Ice (blocks and bags for cooler)

Pie crusts (homebaked or ready-made)

Sandwiches (without mayonnaise or lettuce)

Vegetables

(Unless already packaged for freezing, all foods should be wrapped securely before storing in freezer. Always label with date of storage.)

On the Shelves:

Beverages (cider, fruit juices, mineral waters, punch bases, sodas, wines, assorted teas — loose and bags, black, green and herbal, cocoa, coffee — ground and instant)

Canned brown bread and nut bread

Canned fish (caviar, clams, oysters, salmon, shrimp, sardines, tuna)

Canned fruits

Canned meats (chicken, corned beef, ham, pâté, tongue)

Canned soups and broths, dry packaged soup mixes (for spread and dips)

Canned vegetables (asparagus, beans, tiny beets, mushrooms)

Chocolate chips, baking squares, candy bars

Chips

Crackers

Cookies

Dried fruits

Ethnic specialties (from international markets)

Herbs and spices

Marinated artichoke hearts, bottoms, and mushrooms

Milk (canned and powdered)

Nuts, trail mix snacks, sunflower and pumpkin seeds

Olive oil and salad oil

Olives (ripe, green and stuffed)

Onions, garlic, shallots

Peanut and other nut butters

Pimentos, peppers

Sugar (packets) or honey (in plastic container)

Vinegar

Always ready to go, the English fitted picnic hamper represents the ultimate in portable feast transportation. In lieu of expensive and often hard-to-find commercial baskets, make your own from the directions on the opposite page.

Fitted Picnic Basket

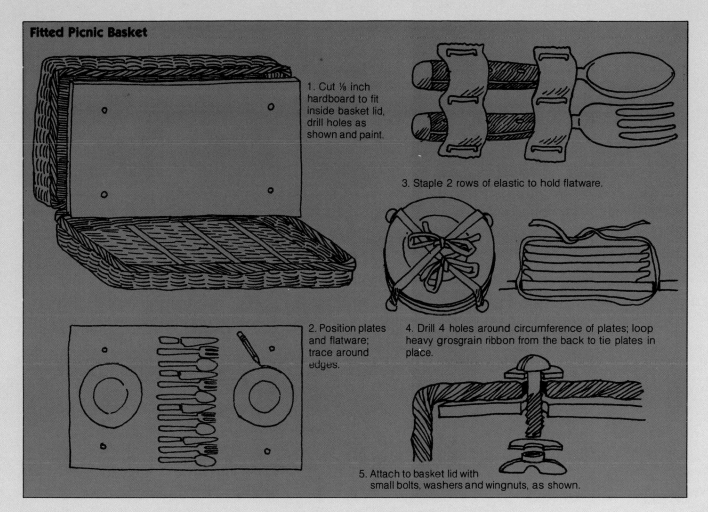

1. Cut ⅛ inch hardboard to fit inside basket lid, drill holes as shown and paint.

3. Staple 2 rows of elastic to hold flatware.

2. Position plates and flatware; trace around edges.

4. Drill 4 holes around circumference of plates; loop heavy grosgrain ribbon from the back to tie plates in place.

5. Attach to basket lid with small bolts, washers and wingnuts, as shown.

A Guide to Nonedible Supplies

Your own common-sense inventiveness will serve as the best guide to picnicking equipment that's right for you. Following are ideas for what works best in most cases. Freely adapt to fit your own particular needs.

Baskets

Wicker baskets or hampers are the traditional picnic carryalls. The top of the basket line is certainly the English-style, flat sided, rectangular hamper with the lid and body fitted with almost everything — flatware, dishes, glasses, napkins, corkscrew, and so on. Luxury models represent picnic packing at its ultimate and cost in the hundreds of dollars. (See page 46.) Less expensive, smaller variations exist and, needless to say, are more popular. An inventive person can create an original version with a large basket, and hardware fittings. (See above.)

Import shops sell baskets made in many different countries. In all price ranges, shapes and sizes, they are often adaptable to carrying food. Select those that are sturdy and substantial, have a lid or cover, strong handles, and plenty of room inside.

There are many alternatives to wicker basketry. For instance, wire baskets from Europe, often found in gourmet cookware shops, are strong and fairly roomy. Use a tablecloth to line the inside; then pack the food. (See page 44.)

Stacking: One type of Chinese basket has several compartments that stack upon each other, held snugly by a handle running from bottom to top. They're excellent for small picnics that don't require a lot of food and utensils.

Japanese lacquerware is compact and beautiful. Compartments keep food separated and double as serving dishes.

Plastic carriers: Check out what's available in plastics. Compact units are fitted with dishes and flatware in modern design, but there's not much room for adding food. Pails and buckets padded with newspapers or towels work well for carrying bottles and small casseroles.

Totes and packs: Canvas totes, duffle bags or luggage pieces are versatile and lightweight. It's amazing how much food and equipment you can stuff inside. Nylon bags and day-hike packs are extremely practical; they're washable and light.

If you sew, construct a tote as shown on page 97, or modify it to any shape you wish for whatever specialized equipment you require, such as a skillet.

There is a handy design for carrying hot dishes, spillable bean pots or casseroles down steep hillsides or long distances. (See page 106.)

Cartons and chests: Heavy-duty recycled cardboard cartons with slots cut for your hands are the readiest means of carrying supplies for large picnics. Lightweight, inexpensive styrofoam ice chests (without the ice) serve the same purpose and the bottoms are somewhat stronger than cardboard. There are fancy cardboad boxes manufactured just for picnickers. One model folds up around lightweight contents to form a built-in handle and at the site opens flat to become a circular tabletop.

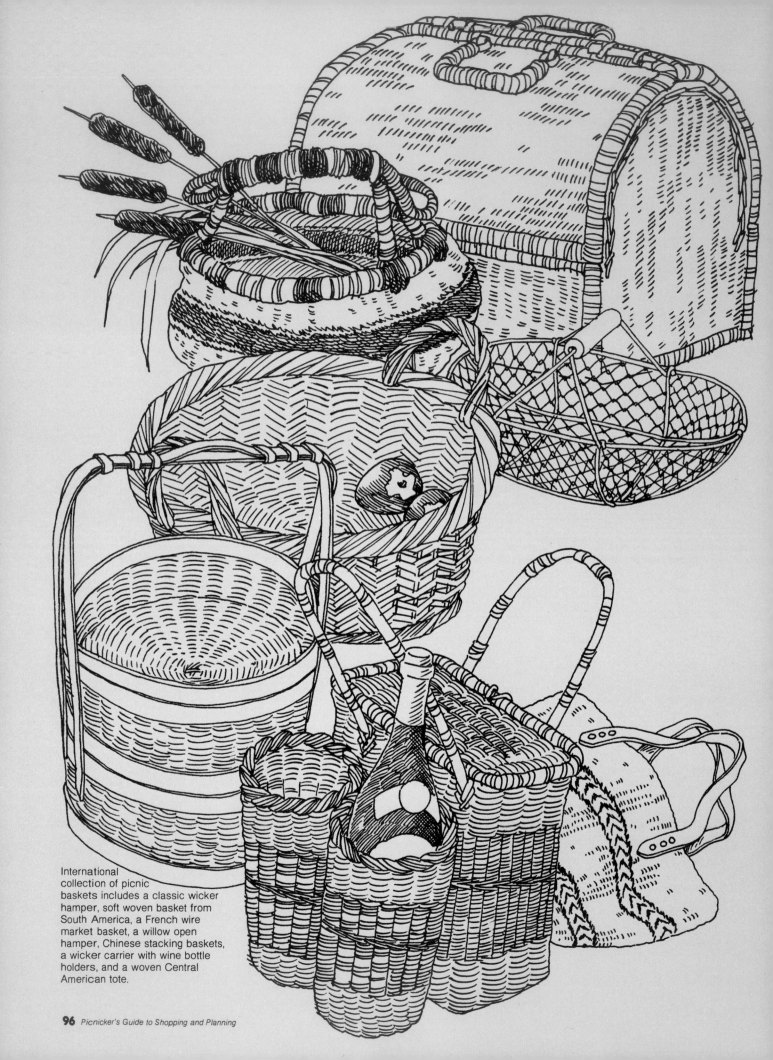

International
collection of picnic
baskets includes a classic wicker
hamper, soft woven basket from
South America, a French wire
market basket, a willow open
hamper, Chinese stacking baskets,
a wicker carrier with wine bottle
holders, and a woven Central
American tote.

Bags: Shopping bags are excellent for holding everything for a simple picnic. In New York it's quite chic to be seen with a famous West Side deli bag packed with food. Save attractive shopping bags for transporting excess items that won't fit into the main picnic hamper.

Ground Covers and Tablecloths

Choose a blanket, patchwork quilt, bedspread, sheet, comforter, afghan, woolen throw or any large piece of fabric for a ground cover-tablecloth. Top it, if you like, with a decorative second cloth that fits the mood of the picnic you've planned.

No-iron cotton or synthetic fabric is easy to keep clean and ready for traveling. Other choices to consider are beach towels, bamboo or reed matting, nylon parachute fabric, flannel shirt material or lengths of any easy-care fabric stitched at each end. East Indian and Mediterranean bedspreads and throws, available at import shops, are inexpensive and colorful for table top or sitting areas. (See page 54.)

Purchase one or two plastic painters' drop cloths or carry a canvas tarpaulin to put down before you spread the tablecloth if the ground is damp, dusty or snow covered.

You may choose to stack individual food containers Japanese style in the middle of a square of fabric, a **furoshiki**, and tie the opposite corners together to form a handle. The **furoshiki** serves as an instant tablecloth when you unpack. (See pages 42 and 99.)

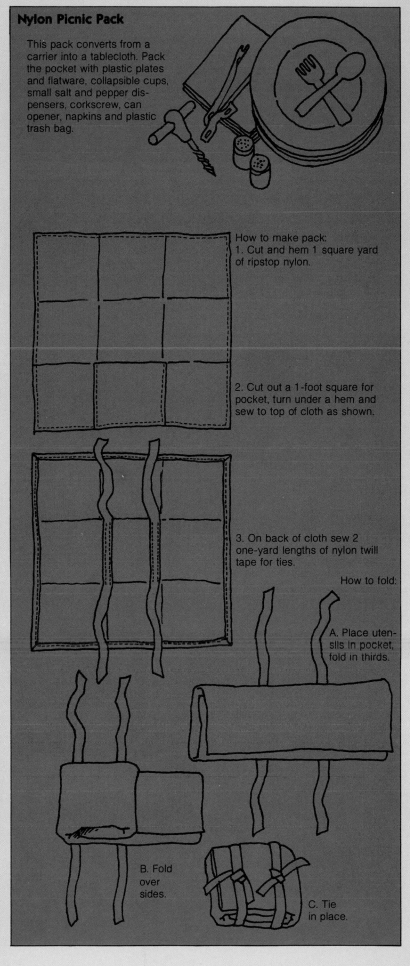

Nylon Picnic Pack

This pack converts from a carrier into a tablecloth. Pack the pocket with plastic plates and flatware, collapsible cups, small salt and pepper dispensers, corkscrew, can opener, napkins and plastic trash bag.

How to make pack:
1. Cut and hem 1 square yard of ripstop nylon.

2. Cut out a 1-foot square for pocket, turn under a hem and sew to top of cloth as shown.

3. On back of cloth sew 2 one-yard lengths of nylon twill tape for ties.

How to fold:

A. Place utensils in pocket, fold in thirds.

B. Fold over sides.

C. Tie in place.

Tables and Chairs

Most picnics are spread upon a blanket or other ground cover, but there are times when a proper table is definitely in order. When you've produced a lavish banquet, you want to give it the support it deserves. If some guests can't or don't enjoy eating at ground level, table-height dining should be provided.

Folding picnic tables come in a variety of styles and prices. Metal frames are best. Use the table in full upright position with legs securely locked in place. Or leave it folded and elevate to a low height atop a steady base of stones, boxes or crates. (See the Mid-East table, page 54.) Some tables have folding sides which can be used as supports for a low table, as shown in the Wine Tasting, page 81. A card table or other small folding table is of great help in getting food to the picnic table. It can be set up near the car as the staging area for transfer of food to serving containers, carving of meats or finishing touch-ups to certain dishes.

To build your own portable table suitable for low seating, saw the legs of an old wooden folding card table to the desired length. Or buy folding legs at a lumberyard and attach to a ¼-inch or ½-inch plywood or Formica-covered table top. A folding army cot fitted with a hinged ¼-inch plywood top is an excellent picnic table. Hinged sections can be folded and tucked into the car trunk — unfold and rest it on the ground when you need a smooth solid surface, or rest it on supports for a taller table. For other tables to build, refer to the Ortho book **Wood Projects for the Garden**.

Lightweight chairs of metal, wood and fabric come in a wide range of styles and colors, many at very low prices. Choose simple slings, armchairs or even chaise lounges. For afternoon napping carry along a lightweight hammock to hang between two trees. Include pillows for lounging.

Simple folding campstools take up such little space, you may decide to leave them in the car trunk for impromptu outings. Shooting sticks, or spectator seats, are sturdy tripod or single-leg supports topped by a folding seat. Look for them in sporting goods stores.

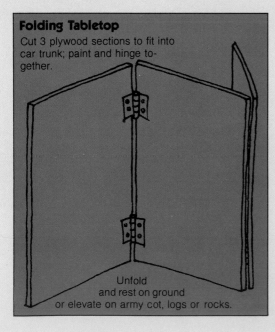

Folding Tabletop

Cut 3 plywood sections to fit into car trunk; paint and hinge together.

Unfold
and rest on ground
or elevate on army cot, logs or rocks.

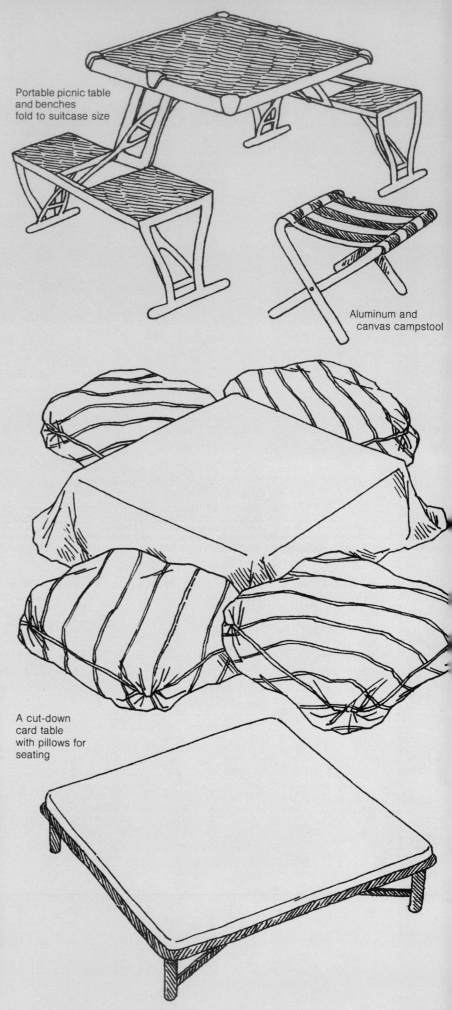

Portable picnic table and benches fold to suitcase size

Aluminum and canvas campstool

A cut-down card table with pillows for seating

Furoshiki

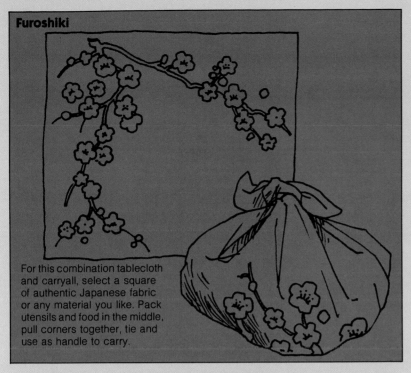

For this combination tablecloth and carryall, select a square of authentic Japanese fabric or any material you like. Pack utensils and food in the middle, pull corners together, tie and use as handle to carry.

Farolito

Night lighting is easy with paper bags turned down to form a collar, then filled ⅓ full with sand to support a candle. Surround the picnic site or mark a trail for guests.

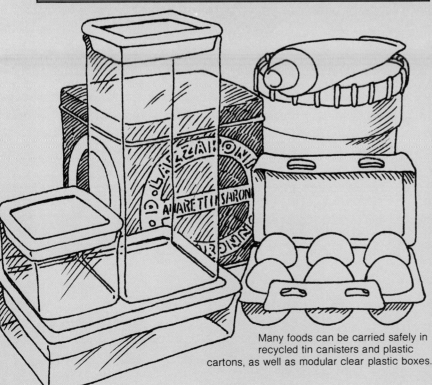

Many foods can be carried safely in recycled tin canisters and plastic cartons, as well as modular clear plastic boxes.

Setting the Table

Table settings for a picnic deserve to be as attractive as they are for any other meal.

Plates: There are picnics that call for best china, but for most occasions you'll want plates that are inexpensive or nonbreakable. You may want to buy dinner or luncheon sizes as well as the smaller salad and dessert size. Consider either round or space-saving square plates made of plastic, tin, enamelware, metal or wood, also. They're long-run money savers compared to paper products.

If you prefer paper plates, look for those that are sturdy, glazed, large and divided into sections. Is there anything worse than eating from a small, soggy, limp plate? However, low-cost flat baskets are available to hold thin paper plates and give them strength. Choose plates in many colors to add variety. Line shallow baskets with sheets of waxed or butcher paper for serving sandwiches, chicken and other finger foods, as some fast-food restaurants do.

Glasses and Cups: Plastic glasses come in a wide range of sizes, styles and colors. They're quite satisfactory for everything from champagne to lemonade, although for special times you'll want to pack proper glasses, even stemware. Cups can be the same material, color and pattern as your plates, or plain heavy-duty coated paper. For hot soups and stews, add insulated mugs, strong glazed paper bowls, or bowls to match the plates. There are mixed feelings about styrofoam cups. You like them or you don't. But, they do keep contents hot.

Flatware: Although many of your meals will consist of finger foods and won't require flatware, habitual picnickers need a set of stainless steel forks, spoons, and knives to keep in the picnic hamper. Or, look for large-scale, plastic flatware in clear, opaque white or bright colors. Chopsticks save a lot of room and can act as serving tools, too. Take along appropriate bowls, trays or other serving pieces, if the food containers won't do for serving. Also, serve from baskets to accent the picnic mood.

Napkins: Cloth napkins add a touch of class and they're less expensive in the long run than their one-time-use paper counterparts. Buy or make napkins of no-iron cotton, linen or other fabric. Easiest to keep up are terrycloth napkins or kitchen towels.

If you choose the paper route, don't just stop with bottom-of-the-line grocery store napkins. There are vibrant colors in paper products to match or contrast with the rest of your table setting. Stock up on matching napkins, tablecloths and plates from stationery stores.

Extras: Include in your collection a vase for flowers and a bowl or basket for fruit. Have candles on hand for dining into the dusk. When it's windy, enclose candles in hurricane shades or inside paper bags half-filled with sand — the **farolito** of the Southwest.

Food Containers

You'll need a supply of multipurpose containers in various sizes for all types of food. Rigid plastic stacking boxes and bowls with tight-sealing lids are really the best. Plastic or glass jars with screw-on lids are ideal for liquids. Remember that square-shaped containers will take less space than round.

Recycled tea canisters, coffee cans and cracker tins are excellent. Also, keep a supply of self-sealing and tie-type plastic bags, foil paper, wax paper or plastic wrap.

Planning a Picnic

Obviously your picnics, especially the big outdoor events, will run more smoothly if you take time to schedule the cooking chores in advance as well as organize the transportation of everything to the picnic site.

Checklist of Picnic Equipment

Inveterate picnickers will include most of the following gear and nonperishable supplies.

Casual, occasional picnickers need to stock only the absolute basics listed in bold face type.

- ☐ **Basket, hamper, tote or carryall**
- ☐ Plastic or canvas groundcloth
- ☐ Plastic food containers or plastic wraps and bags, various sizes
- ☐ **Tablecloth**
- ☐ **Mess kits: plastic or metal (instead of separate plates, cups, flatware)**
- ☐ **Napkins: paper or cloth**
- ☐ Glasses: plastic or glass
- ☐ Cups: plastic, enamelware, styrofoam
- ☐ Plates: plastic, paper, ceramic
- ☐ Flatware: plastic or stainless steel
- ☐ Serving spoons
- ☐ **Can and bottle openers**
- ☐ **Corkscrew**
- ☐ **Thermoses, several shapes and sizes, or plastic flasks**
- ☐ **Cooler or ice chest**
  (Always use a cooler to carry food that normally is refrigerated.)
- ☐ Folding table
- ☐ Moist towelettes for cleanup
- ☐ Paper towels
- ☐ **Knives: paring and bread slicing**
- ☐ Small cutting board
- ☐ Salt, pepper, sugar or honey, coffee creamer, mustard and catsup in airtight containers
- ☐ Folding stove, hibachi or other portable heating source
- ☐ Fuel and matches
- ☐ Insect repellent
- ☐ Flashlight
- ☐ Portable seating: folding chairs or stools
- ☐ Temporary shelter for shade or from rain, wind
- ☐ Vase or jar for flowers
- ☐ **Extra paper or plastic bag for cleanup**

The success of a picnic often rests on a dependable corkscrew and bottle opener, or the versatile Swiss army knife.

Epicurean cookware departments in stores such as New York's Bloomingdales are bonanzas for picnic shoppers.

Planning the Extravaganza

Nearly any picnic requires a basic checklist of what you plan to take, but full-scale events necessitate detailed organization. Arm yourself with common-sense plans: one, a day-to-day schedule; two, a master checklist.

Prepare as much food as possible in advance. Many items can be made a week or more before the big day and frozen or refrigerated until packing time. Following is an example of the food preparation schedule for our Thanksgiving Feast shown on page 10. The Wedding Pot Luck Picnic, page 23, and the Latin Fiesta, page 51, require similar planning.

Thanksgiving Food Preparation Schedule

(**Menu:** Smoked clams, mussels, oysters; Lobster bisque; Orange-glazed roast ducklings; Baked corn; Molded cranberry relish; Biscuits; Pumpkin bread; Strawberry jam and Plum jelly; Persimmon pudding and Hard sauce; Mincemeat pie; Red and white wines; Herbal tea)

A week or more ahead
- ☐ Make master lists for food and equipment
- ☐ Bake pumpkin bread, mincemeat pie, persimmon pudding; freeze
- ☐ Purchase smoked seafoods, jams, jelly, wines and other nonperishables

Two or three days before
- ☐ Complete shopping
- ☐ Pack table service and equipment in labeled boxes or bags

Day before
Prepare and refrigerate:
- ☐ Molded cranberry relish
- ☐ Lobster bisque
- ☐ Hard sauce
- ☐ Biscuit dough
- ☐ Thaw pumpkin bread, mincemeat pie, persimmon pudding, and refrigerate

Thanksgiving morning
- ☐ Roast ducklings; wrap in foil, then in newspapers to keep warm
- ☐ Bake corn in casserole; wrap in foil
- ☐ Bake biscuits; place in foil-wrapped basket or thermal container
- ☐ Bake acorn squash; wrap individually in foil, then in newspapers
- ☐ Reheat lobster bisque, pour into thermos jug
- ☐ Wrap bread, pies and pudding in plastic wrap; place in cartons for carrying
- ☐ Place in ice chest: cranberry mold covered with plastic wrap, hard sauce in covered bowl, white wine, milk and butter.
- ☐ Check master list and pack remaining items in labeled cartons and bags
- ☐ Load car

Master List

Before setting off on any full-scale outing, make a master list of everything you'll require for packing and transporting food, for cooling or heating foods to desired temperatures, for creating the setting, serving and eating. Here's the list for our Thanksgiving picnic.

Thanksgiving Picnic Checklist
- ☐ Folding table, if site doesn't have permanent tables
- ☐ Folding stools
- ☐ Patchwork quilts for tablecover and seating
- ☐ Plastic dropcloth in case of rain
- ☐ Plates and saucers, heavy duty paper
- ☐ Napkins, cloth
- ☐ Mugs for bisque
- ☐ Styrofoam cups for tea
- ☐ Plastic wine glasses
- ☐ Flatware: knives, forks, teaspoons, serving spoons
- ☐ Carving set for ducklings
- ☐ Serving baskets, trays, bowls for each dish on menu
- ☐ Water in thermos jug for drinking and cleanup
- ☐ Wide-mouth thermos for bisque
- ☐ Portable stove, fuel, matches
- ☐ Kettle for boiling tea water
- ☐ Saucepan for reheating bisque
- ☐ Table decorations: chrysanthemums, ornamental gourds, Indian corn and fruit

For Thanksgiving dinner we carried plastic wine glasses, styrofoam cups for tea and ceramic soup mugs.

Table decorations included gourds, Indian corn, squash and a pumpkin.

Smoked turkey was the highlight of a family patio get-together. Figure ½ pound of smoked meats per person.

Left: Ice cream loving guests consumed quite a few gallons in various flavors at our hot summer supersundae. Above: It was so cold at our cross country ski picnic that food was eaten in haste.

Feeding a Crowd: 50 or 10

The following amounts will serve crowds of 50 or 10. Multiply or divide for more or less. (These are only suggested amounts; vary according to anticipated appetites of guests, size of servings and availability of items.)

Food:	50	10
Bread	4 loaves	1 loaf
Butter	1½ pounds	½ pound
Cakes	3	1
Cantaloupes	25	5
Cheese	5 pounds	1 pound
Chickens	13-25	3-5
Corn	50 ears	10 ears
Beef ribs	75 pounds	15 pounds
Ham, boneless	14 pounds	3 pounds
Hamburger	13 pounds	2½ pounds
Ice cream	3-4 gallons	1 gallon
Lettuce	12 heads	1-2 heads
Olives	2 quarts	1 pint
Rolls	75-100	15-20
Pies	9	2
Potatoes	15 pounds	3 pounds
Soup	5 gallons	1 gallon
Vegetables	3 gallons	½ gallon

Beverages:	50	10
Coffee	7 cups ground coffee	1 cup ground coffee
	12 quarts water	2½ quarts water
Cocoa	2 cups unsweetened cocoa	½ cup unsweetened cocoa
	2-2½ cups sugar	½-1 cup sugar
	½ teaspoon salt	Pinch salt
	1 quart boiling water	1 cup boiling water
	10 quarts warm milk	2½ quarts warm milk
Lemonade	3 dozen lemons	8-9 lemons
	4 cups sugar	¾-1 cup sugar
	11 quarts cold water	3 quarts cold water
	Ice	Ice
Iced tea	1½ cups loose tea	⅛-½ cup loose tea
	2½ quarts boiling water	2½ cups boiling water
	6 quarts cold water	1½ quarts cold water
	Ice	Ice

Large pot luck gatherings have been a part of the picnic scene through the years.

Packing, Transporting and Safe-Storing Tips
Packing to go

■ Prepare all food as close to departure time as comfortably possible for you. Don't cook in advance earlier than the time recommended in the recipe, unless the item can be frozen successfully.

■ Whenever possible, pack your hamper or other carryall in reverse order from the way in which you'll use the items at the site: food on the bottom; then serving items and tableware; finally, tablecloth on top.

■ Always place food containers right side up to prevent spills and breakage. Leaking foods can ruin everything in your hamper. If tops of containers do not fit securely, reinforce them with a band of masking tape around the lid. Play it very safe and put jars or bowls that might leak inside heavy-duty plastic bags, secure the top of the bag with tape, twist ties or rubber bands.

■ Breakable glassware can be wrapped in the tablecloth, napkins, kitchen towels, paper towels or newspaper. Separate breakable items with plastic containers or soft goods when filling the ham-

per. Wrap fragile items well and place in a separate container to be held while traveling.

■ Foods, such as pies, tarts, cakes, muffins, mousses, molded salads or homebaked breads that crumble easily, can be carried in the pans in which they were prepared. At time of baking, cakes and bread are turned out to cool, then slipped back into their pans and wrapped in foil for protection en route. Coffee cans are handy to bake in and easy to carry. At the picnic, just open the bottom of the can with a can opener and push out the bread or cake. Use masking tape to hold springform pans (with removable bottoms) in place while traveling. Very fragile tarts or quiches can remain in their pans with a slightly larger pan inverted over the top. Secure with masking tape and wrap both pans tightly together with foil. (Consider carrying along the frosting separately for simple cakes baked in flat pans. Frost at picnic site.)

■ Don't leave vacant spots in the picnic hamper or box. If the supplies do not fill the container, fill in with rolled newspaper or paper towels to prevent foods from overturning or bumping together.

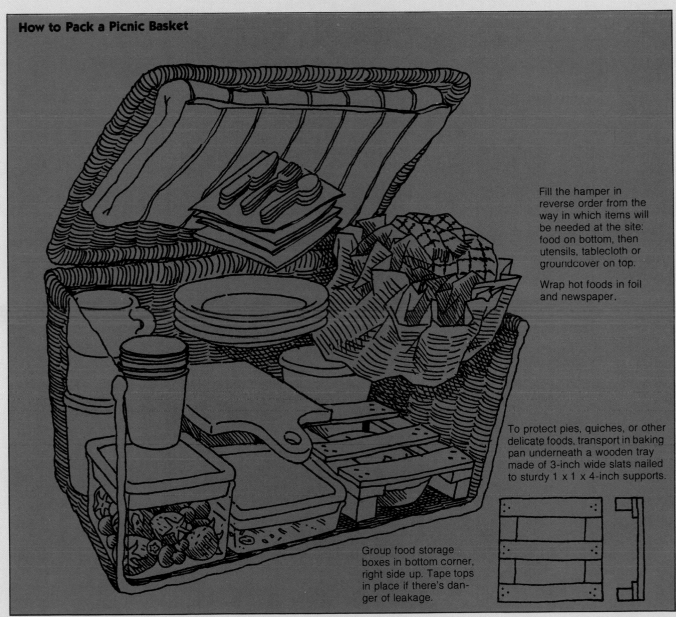

How to Pack a Picnic Basket

Fill the hamper in reverse order from the way in which items will be needed at the site: food on bottom, then utensils, tablecloth or groundcover on top.

Wrap hot foods in foil and newspaper.

To protect pies, quiches, or other delicate foods, transport in baking pan underneath a wooden tray made of 3-inch wide slats nailed to sturdy 1 x 1 x 4-inch supports.

Group food storage boxes in bottom corner, right side up. Tape tops in place if there's danger of leakage.

Hot and Cold Storage Equipment

Coolers: If you carry a lot of chilled food or use a cooler often, invest in the most heavily insulated metal chest you can find; now-and-then revelers can make do with one of the inexpensive plastic or styrofoam types.

There are also small coolers designed to hold only a six-pack of drinks with ice cubes. If your outing is to be a short distance away and you only have a few items that need to stay cool, pack them inside a zippered or drawstring-tied insulated bag and add a plastic bag of ice cubes.

There are permanently sealed refrigerant blocks you can keep in the freezer between picnics. They are around 10 degrees colder than ice and handy because they don't melt and make a mess as ice does.

Cookers: Folding stoves, hibachis and bucket broilers are indispensible for reheating soup, making coffee or tea on the site or doing simple picnic cookery. Many people have found through experience that a folding campstove is worth the initial investment — it's easy to carry, set up and use, and takes up little storage space. You also may wish to purchase a folding grill designed for a campfire. Whatever heating device you choose, be sure to keep charcoal or fuel supply on hand at home, along with a waterproof container of kitchen matches. Sterno, denatured alcohol or candles are necessary for chafing dishes or fondue sets.

Thermoses: Collect several shapes and sizes. In addition to the regular sizes for hot and cold liquids, select a super-large version for ice water, drinks or foods for a crowd. Add a couple of wide-mouth types for soups, stews and other chunky foods. If you picnic alone or by twos, consider individual-size thermoses.

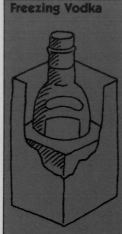
Keeping Foods Cold

■ The length of time in which food can spoil is relative. It depends not only on how hot the weather is, but also upon the way the food was cooked, chilled, wrapped and carried. Foods containing mayonnaise, eggs, cream, sour cream, yogurt or fish are safe unrefrigerated up to 2 hours, **if the weather is fairly cool.** If it will be more than 2 hours before you eat, plan to carry along a refrigerated cooler. Cool dishes as quickly as possible after preparing them and leave them in the refrigerator until just before time to leave.

■ Remember this cardinal rule: **Never take anything on a picnic that could possibly spoil unless you can provide effective portable refrigeration.**

■ Ice chests or coolers can be chilled with ice cubes, crushed or chipped ice, blocks from ice machines, blocks frozen in clean milk cartons or other containers.

■ Fill plastic bottles (with lids) 2/3 full with water to allow for expansion and freeze overnight. These frozen containers eliminate the mess of melted ice. Fruit juice in plastic bottles can also be frozen ahead and used in the cooler. Juice will thaw readily when needed.

■ Dry ice may also be used in coolers. Place it on top of foods so that the chilling carbon dioxide, heavier than air, travels downward. Wrap dry ice in several layers of paper; never place it unwrapped in the cooler.

■ Permanently sealed refrigerant blocks are very handy. They are several degrees colder than ice, can be kept in the freezer between picnics and don't melt as ice does.

■ Store cold drinks on the bottom with foods on top or in a separate compartment if the cooler is divided.

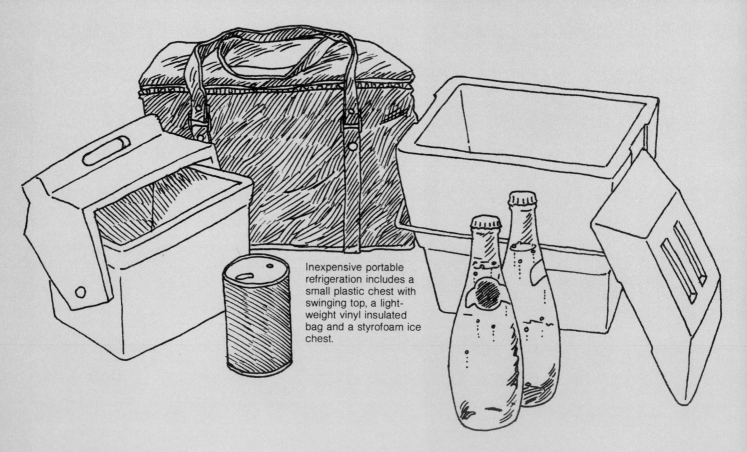

Inexpensive portable refrigeration includes a small plastic chest with swinging top, a light-weight vinyl insulated bag and a styrofoam ice chest.

■ You can count on heavily insulated metal coolers to keep foods sufficiently cold from 24 to 48 hours. Inexpensive styrofoam coolers work well for much shorter periods, depending on weather and amount of ice. Open all ice chests as little as possible after filling; never allow to stand open. Find a shady place for the cooler during the picnic; cover it with a blanket, beach towels or tarpaulin.

■ It's a good idea to transport mayonnaise in small containers in an ice chest, then add to salads or spread on sandwiches at the site.

■ Whipped cream can be transported in a sealed plastic jar or bowl in the cooler; or take a wire whisk to whip cream at the picnic.

■ Combine rinsed, dried, torn and chilled salad greens in a plastic bowl or bag that seals; keep chilled in cooler. Carry dressing in a separate container and toss salad at the last minute. Pack watercress, parsley, mint, grapes, lemon slices and other garnishes in sealed bags for finishing dishes on-site.

■ There are times when you'll want to chill foods just to improve taste. Don't bother with the cooler — just place beverages, well-sealed containers or unopened canned foods in a plastic bag and partially sink in a cool stream.

■ Add cold foods or liquids to thermoses that have been chilled with ice water or placed in the refrigerator for an hour. Foods will stay cold from several hours to all day, depending on the weather and how often you open the container.

How to Pack an Ice Chest

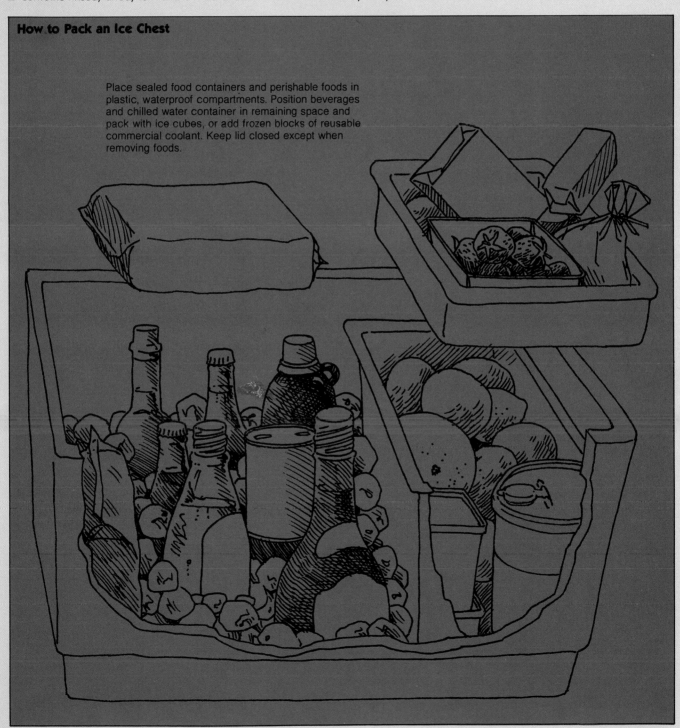

Place sealed food containers and perishable foods in plastic, waterproof compartments. Position beverages and chilled water container in remaining space and pack with ice cubes, or add frozen blocks of reusable commercial coolant. Keep lid closed except when removing foods.

Keeping Foods Hot

■ Styrofoam and insulated chests and ice buckets can be used to keep foods hot, too. Carry in them very hot, foil-wrapped pots of beans, stews or other such foods. Stuff empty spaces with rolled newspaper and cover securely.

■ To carry hot foods in dutch ovens, casseroles or bean pots, wrap the thoroughly heated container in heavy-duty aluminum foil and several thicknesses of newspaper. Place in box or carrier. Food will remain hot for 2 to 4 hours.

■ Construct an insulated bag to line a basket. Use insulation material (available at hardware stores) sewn securely inside a double plastic bag, as shown. A drawstring top over an inserted pad keeps heat trapped inside for several hours.

■ Thermosware should be heated or chilled to the same temperature as its contents. Before adding piping hot liquids or foods, heat the thermos with boiling water and drain. Contents will stay hot all day.

■ Before filling any thermos, check to be sure the glass liner is intact. A gentle shake will tell you if the liner is broken. Stainless steel thermoses and liners are heavy and do not keep contents hot as long as others, but they are virtually indestructible!

Casserole Tote

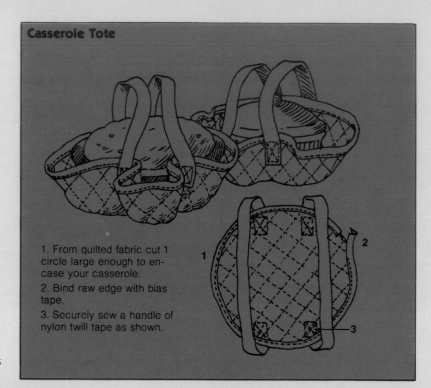

1. From quilted fabric cut 1 circle large enough to encase your casserole.

2. Bind raw edge with bias tape.

3. Securely sew a handle of nylon twill tape as shown.

Insulated Basket

1. Measure depth and circumference of basket. Cut paper-covered insulation material to size. Cut heavy plastic 1½-inches larger on all sides. Completely encase insulation in plastic and sew as shown. Cut opening on both sides of top edge for drawstring.

2. Cut 2 circles to fit top and bottom; encase in plastic.

3. Run sturdy cord through top casing for drawstring. Fit rectangle into basket. Put in bottom circle.

4. Fill basket. Put top in place and cinch up drawstring.

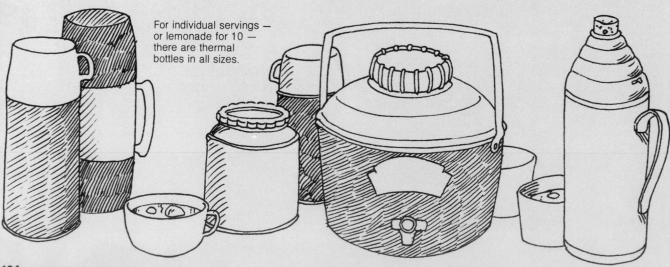

For individual servings — or lemonade for 10 — there are thermal bottles in all sizes.

Taking It Home

■ Try to avoid leftovers by careful planning for the number of people expected. But if there is food you want to bring home, wrap as soon as possible with the same care as packing for the trip out. Place perishables in ice chest immediately.

■ **Throw away any picnic food left over if there is the slightest doubt as to its safety.**

■ For further information on food spoilage and safety, order a copy of **Keeping Foods Safe to Eat,** Publications Division, Office of Government and Public Affairs, U.S. Department of Agriculture, Washington, D.C. 20025.

Wieners dropped into boiling water inside a wide-mouth thermos just before leaving home will be plump and ready to serve when you arrive at the picnic site.

Wrapping a Hot Dish

Wrap covered hot Dutch oven, casserole, or other container in a dishtowel, then foil and several layers of newspaper. Carry in closed cardboard box.

For heating foods at the picnic site consider taking along a charcoal burning hibachi, folding campstove or portable barbecue grill. If there is an electrical source, take along one of the new lightweight convection ovens or a small microwave oven.

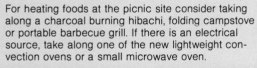

The Picnic Site

This book is filled with photographs suggesting places to picnic, from the obvious to the imaginative.

Wherever you choose to go, you must always secure permission to picnic on private land, and more and more frequently on public lands. Many parks require a small fee for the use of picnic facilities. If you plan a big event for a large group of people at a state, city or other public park, call ahead and reserve a space several days in advance. Often, city parks will reserve or rent certain areas for groups. Check with your local park department.

When picnicking on the beach or in the wilds, acquaint yourself with any local regulations regarding swimming, fishing and gathering seafood or wildflowers. Be sure that you do not pick fruits or berries or take other property.

Some picnickers enjoy gathering edible wild greens for salads. **Do this only if you can be absolutely sure of the plant's identity.** Picnickers also should learn to identify and avoid poisonous plants and snakes. It is wise always to carry along a simple first aid kit and a snake bite kit and how to use it. Observe caution when you gather wood or hike. Courses in wildlife and plant identification

Securing Poles

Here are two ways to anchor bamboo poles or dowels for flying site markers shown below.

1. With a hammer, drive a slim metal rod into the ground, leaving 10 to 12 inches exposed; force hollow bamboo pole over rod.

2. Or drive a 2-foot long pipe into the ground; insert pole or dowel into pipe.

are usually available through local adult education programs. Learn as much as possible about the natural life in your corner of the world.

Follow common-sense rules of safety when you build a fire or use a portable stove. If you build a campfire, be sure it is completely out when you finish by covering the embers with several inches of sand or soil.

Note: In many areas, a fire permit is required and may be obtained from a ranger or other official.

The most important thing to remember about the picnic site is to follow the picnicker's golden rule and always leave the site as you'd like to find it. Place all refuse in trash bins if they're available. Carry away every speck of litter, beverage can rings and broken glass. Picnic fans, perhaps more than some, appreciate the splendid backdrops nature has provided for outdoor feasts. Deep respect for the environment requires us to take a personal responsibility for its care and maintenance.

Opposite: Along with a beautiful site, good food and pleasant company, be sure to add activity and fun to your creative picnic planning.

Create festive picnic sites with purchased or homecrafted banners, pennants.

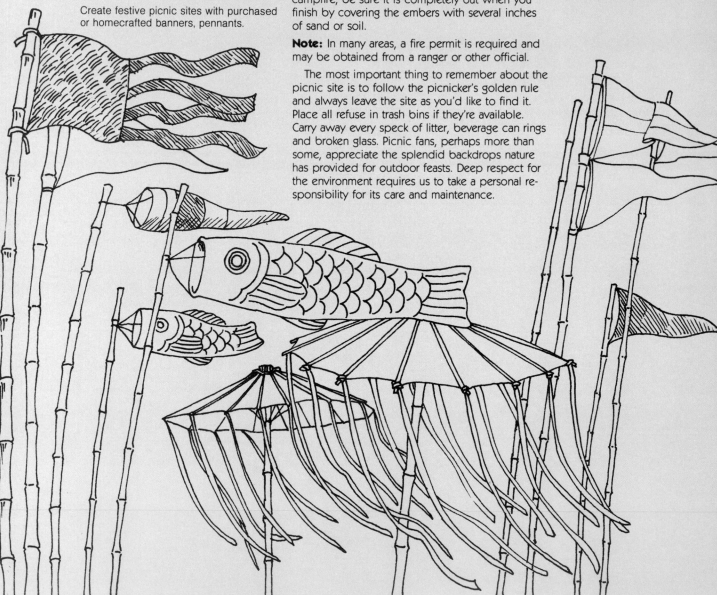

Index

Acknowledgements

Research and Background:
Karen Evans
Ellen Sugarman

Appreciation from the author to the following for sharing ideas, recipes and time:
Matilda Adams
Dante Barboni
Michael Bird
Sharon Blondell
Mrs. T.E. Buckles,
 Devereaux Plantation
Eula Cain
Chevron USA Magazine
Chrystine Conn
Ruth Dosher
Golden Gate Park,
 San Francisco
Cary Griffin
Helen and Ronald
 Johnson
Olivia Bell Keith
Michael Landis
Pat Latimer and Sherry
 Institute of Spain
Le Pique Nique
Al Lovi and Petrini's
 Maison Gourmet
George Marsh
J.O. and Lucille McNair
Novack Vineyard
Jose Pons
Adrian Prattini
Terry Robinson
Samuel P. Taylor State
 Park, CA.
San Francisco
 Zoological Gardens
Leslie Sarfert
Will Webber

Special Consultant:
Lin Cotton
 Picnic Productions
 International, Inc.,
 San Francisco

Crafts and Illustrations:
Designed by
Alan May

Photography Credits:
Tom Tracy: Front cover, Back cover - top and lower left, 1, 3, 4, 5, 8, 10, 11, 12, 13, 16-top, 20, 26, 29-bottom, 32, 33, 37, 38, 39, 41, 42, 43, 44, 45, 46, 47, 48, 49, 50-51, 52, 53, 56, 57, 58-top, 62, 66, 67-right, 68, 69, 71, 72-73, 75, 79, 84, 85-bottom, 86, 87, 88, 89, 90, 93, 94, 97, 102-middle, 109

Dennis Bettencourt: 18, 22, 24, 34, 35, 54, 64, 65, 81, 83-top, 91

Robin Forbes: 77-bottom

Louis Hicks: Back cover-lower right

Fred Kaplan: 23-right, 60, 61, 67-left, 70, 76-bottom, 77-top, 105

Marian May: 78

James K. McNair: 6, 19, 21, 23-left, 28, 29-top, 30, 31, 36, 40, 83-bottom, 85-top, 102-top

Dick Rowan: 9, 14, 15, 16-bottom, 17, 27, 58-bottom, 59, 63, 76-top, 80, 82

James Stockton: 100

Photographic Research:
Carousel-Winfrey
Page 6—Culver Pictures, Manet-Louvre, Granger Collection
Page 102-Bottom—Culver Pictures

Props for Photography:
Forrest Jones, San Francisco, most of the items shown throughout the book;
City Island, San Francisco, spreads and tablecloths on pages 22, 50-51, 54;
Dandelion, San Francisco, pages 64 and 71;
Etc. Etc. Etc., San Francisco, small penguins on pages 72-73;
I. Magnin, San Francisco, large penguins on pages 72-73;
Istanbul, San Francisco, copper pieces on page 54;
Jim Kelly, San Francisco, Bentley automobile, on pages 45, 46;
Outdoors-In, Mill Valley, CA, baskets for illustrations;
Tiffany and Company, San Francisco and New York, pages 46, 72-73

Additional Styling:
Linda Hinrichs, page 68
Charlotte Walker, page 58-top

The Picnickers:
Thanks to the picnickers who appear throughout this book:
Susan Adams
Reina Barone
Jay Baughman
Max Bedel
Vince Beggs
Craig Bergquist
Dennis Bettencourt
Dawn, Joel and Sharon
 Blondell
Alissa and Candy Bly
Ann and Mike Bolton
Angela and Cynthia
 Borcich
Gwen Buford
Greg Burns
Stephanie Breier
Eula Cain
Dorothy Carnal
Linda Catron
Clarence Charles
Sherry Charles
Michael Chauvin
Scott Chiles
Chrystine Conn
Jack Conybear
Jean Corey
Lin Cotton
Richard Dahlberg
Charles Deaton
Peter Devoluy
Christine Dunham
Fred Fox
Arthur Ganger
Yvan Gubler
Mark Herman
Brian, Jeff and Louis
 Hicks
Christine, Gail, Tad,
 Tania and Trip High
Freya, Ingrid, Ron and
 Sally Hildebrand
Kit and Linda Hinrichs
Colleen and David
 Hutcheson
Steven Jensen
Dawn, Helen, Laine and
 Ronald Johnson
George Jones
Jackie Jones
Doris, Olivia and
 Sandford Keith
Jim Kelly
Cathy Kiesecker
Alan Kline
Steve Kubelka
Joshua, Mary and
 Michael Landis and Yo
Lee and Touzette
 LaRavia
Weyman Lew
Edward Lupper
Judy Lusic
Wendy Lynch
Shirley Manning
Rose and Stephan
 Marcus
Alan, Marian and
 Nancy May
Candace McCulloch
J. O., Lucille and
 Martha McNair
Lenny Meyer
Richard Miller
Karen Neal
Peter Olsen
Matilda Parenti
Tom Peinovich
Jason, Judy, Michael
 and Roger Pillon and
 Farfel
Lamar Poole
Joseph Reeves
Steven Reiss
Dart and Dottye Rinefort
Terry Robinson
Claudia and Dick Rowan
Bill and Jean Saylor
Christine and Cori
 Scherer
Vickie Shamlian
Mona Simpson
Cort and Katie Sinnes
Sara Slavin
Al Smith
Dianne Stearns
James Stockton
Ellen Sugarman
Georgia and Henry
 Taliaferro
Barbara and Tom Tracy
Deborah Tubre
Karen Tucker
Bob Turner
Inga Vesik
John Vinton
Judith Whipple
Keetja, Tai,
 Min Lorentz
 and Min S. Yee
Dennis Ziebel
Ellen Zuckerman
and children from
 George Washington
 Elementary School,
 Daly City, California